WELFARE BRAT

WELFARE BRAT

a memoir

MARY CHILDERS

BLOOMSBURY

Published by Bloomsbury Publishing, New York and London
Distributed to the trade by Holtzbrinck Publishers

All papers used by Bloomsbury Publishing are natural, recyclable
products made from wood grown in well-managed forests.
The manufacturing processes conform to the environmental
regulations of the country of origin.

Library of Congress Cataloging-in-Publication Data

Childers, Mary, 1952–
Welfare brat : a memoir / Mary Childers.—1st U.S. ed.
p. cm.
ISBN 1-58234-586-4
ISBN-13 978-1-58234-586-4
1. Childers, Mary, 1952– —Childhood and youth. 2. Childers, Mary,
1952– —Family. 3. Bronx (New York, N.Y.)—Biography. 4. Bronx (New
York, N.Y.)—Social conditions—20th century. 5. Women, White—New
York (State)—New York—Biography. 6. Welfare recipients—New York
(State)—New York—Biography. 7. Urban poor—New York (State)—New
York—Biography. 8. Inner cities—New York (State)—New York. 9. New
York (N.Y.)—Biography. 10. New York (N.Y.)—Social conditions—20th
century. I. Title.

F128.68.B8C48 2005
974.7'275043'092—dc22
2004020999

First U.S. Edition 2005

1 3 5 7 9 10 8 6 4 2

Typeset by Hewer Text Ltd, Edinburgh
Printed in the United States of America
by Quebecor World Fairfield

CONTENTS

PREFACE

One of my nieces is pregnant again, but I am the one roiling inside with mourning sickness. Lisa already has two kids she cannot support, emotionally or financially. She's repeating the mistakes of her mother (my sister Jackie) and her grandmother (my mother). I fear she'll end up begging for welfare and put herself and her kids through the same humiliation that soured my childhood and my mother's life.

There are times when I regard members of my own family as if I'm one of those disgruntled taxpayers who imagine welfare recipients living lives of ease and vice. They think most welfare moms do drugs, drop out of school, spend money on hair dye and cigarettes rather than milk for the kids and have multiple babies with men who shirk both marriage and employment. A lot of people are ready to push women on welfare into the work world even if that means their children will wander unsupervised through our cities' meanest streets. These derelicts can't be

helped, people tell themselves, and close their wallets. I understand their attitude. Why do some poor women replicate mistakes they surely hear others operatically lament? Oh yes, I, too,
sometimes want to confront women who wedge children into the
world without having the resources to care for them.

How could my niece do this to the two children she already
has? Why should her daughters learn that even an unwise
pregnancy makes you the center of so much loving attention?
A mother ought to demonstrate to her children, impressionable
as they are, that reproduction can be controlled. Her daughters
will spend much of their adolescence riven by guilty resentment
and helpless love for that needy baby.

How could she do this to herself? Although she loves her
children, she has often regretted the loss of her youth to them.
Just when she could taste freedom, she may have slipped into
believing the myth that you can keep a man by hatching him a
baby. He fled, of course. She repeated to herself the distorted,
harsh lessons of her own life, her mother's life and her grandmother's life. Sex is a drive that makes your life crash; men are
irresistible scum. Instead of being supported by male companion-
ship and income, she will nurse an infant and also wipe drool off
the chins of Alzheimer's patients for close to minimum wage.

How could she do this to her mother, one of my five sisters,
who lives with her in order to share expenses and childcare? At
fifty-four, Jackie will have to grandmother yet another squealing
bundle of joy when she comes home exhausted after a day of
scrambling for survival wages. Her grandchildren's love and
dependence sustain her, no doubt. Without them, she'd drift
home to an empty apartment, which she would fill primarily with

the sounds of television and plumes of smoke. But after raising her own kids alone and assisting her daughter, she was looking forward to enjoying evenings without a baby tugging at her sleeve—and her heart.

Ah hell, the truth is, I wonder how she could do this to Alice and me. Years ago my sister Alice and I started trying to help Lisa and her kids. If the kids wear serviceable sneakers and enroll in day camp in the summer, if someone buys them books and teaches them early on how to eat in a restaurant or be excited to learn about flora and fauna, maybe, just maybe, they won't drop out of school, use drugs, bear unwanted children. Maybe their childhoods will be less difficult than ours if we launch a rescue and prevention mission.

I question my niece's behavior, but I also empathize with her. The limited involvement of most men in child-rearing and the lack of quality affordable childcare force Lisa to choose between spending time with her kids and earning something resembling a living. While working, she is haunted by what she learned early in her own life: unsupervised children are highly vulnerable. What a heroine you have to be to drag yourself out of bed day after day into minimum-wage jobs, aware that you'll never get ahead and fearful that everything will collapse. No wonder she may have hoped again that love would subsidize her life. Now, with abortion out of the question because of her religious beliefs, she will of course give birth to another cherished obstacle. The child is an excuse, an accident, a gift and a burden.

Lisa's choices mimic those of her mother and her grand-mother. My six siblings and I grew up haphazardly loved and sometimes punished for being alive because our mother, except for being white, fit the stereotype of a welfare queen, reviled by herself, politicians and the general public. Such a queen may breed needy, unwise brats, it is true, but she also raises future citizens like all others—flawed and aspiring toward something better. Our lives have been shadowed by minimal and missed opportunities, too many mistakes, misalliances and miserable memories. Yet, over time, a sense of possibility has emerged. Several of us are thriving and able to help others survive because we refuse to accept family habits and inherited disadvantages as if they are destiny.

1

CHERRY PIE

Three kids clamber to the door as soon as they hear the key turning. Mom must be home, she's come home without stopping at a bar.

"Jesus Christ, can't I have a moment's peace?" is her teasing greeting to the hungry girls circling her, trying to read her face: Is this Good Mom or Evil Mom?

It's Good Mom! She has decided not to complain and won't ignore us by hovering over her two-year-old son, who lives in the playpen.

It's four o'clock on a weekday, which means free school lunch was four hours ago. We've run out of Wonder Bread, which we toast with sugar and butter. It's the third week of November 1962, so the blocks of government surplus cheddar cheese and tins of peanut butter welfare families in the Bronx can pick up at the beginning of the month are long gone. We circle the mother bird, beaks open, chirping and pleading. Today she is not going to take flight from us.

After flinging her coat on top of a dresser, Mom dramatically plops down into one of the torn vinyl kitchen chairs while shaking the big pockets of her waitress apron. We hear the music of change clanging against the chromed metal tubing of the chairs and are ready for what follows her return from the lunchtime shift in midtown Manhattan, where she works off the books two or three days a week to buy more than she can with a welfare check. We know that working is a form of cheating and relish being part of her conspiracy. Pulling an ashtray toward herself, she announces that it is time to start thinking about dinner. "Where are my little pickpockets?" she asks in a loud sing-song voice, hoping Jackie, my fourteen-year-old sister, will rouse herself from one of her notorious marathon naps. Alice, who's four, Joan, who's eight and Mary—that's me—giggle as we empty Mom's pockets, tickling her when a coin is tucked into a corner she is sitting on. Mom loves to have a good time, tickled by us, by beer, by some strange man. Today she is ours.

Carefully stacking towers of pennies, nickels, dimes and quarters, I am resolved to demonstrate my math skills, proud that at ten I can count better than my older sisters. Mom doesn't notice my neat piles. Instead she concentrates on the story behind the five-dollar bill she whips out of the pocket of her blouse. "That's right, it was just three guys having sandwiches and coffee. Their bill was only eight bucks. I told them the one about the mick priest and the rabbi in the bowling alley, and they left me a five. I guess I'm not such an old bag after all."

Calculations finished, I volunteer to shop. Eleven dollars all together means we can buy meat for dinner and two different types of vegetables. "Get some potatoes also and . . ." She teases us by sliding out of her shoes and slipping them back on again, sliding out and slipping in. Barefoot, she sashays over to her coat and fishes through one pocket, then another, miraculously producing more bills. Our beautiful mom proclaims, "Cherry pie from the sky," as she waves and then flings a pack of bills. Four more dollars! She isn't holding anything back to sneak out for beer tonight.

Joan's job is to accompany me to the grocery store and then ceremoniously unveil the cherry pie back home. I am close to two years older than she is and very much in charge. I take advantage. "You look like a string bean, so you should like string beans," I taunt as I grab a large can off the shelves. Hot dogs, potatoes, string beans, creamed corn and cherry pie. Still, there will be change. We prowl down the aisle crammed with once fresh fruit and vegetables. Bananas cost an arm and a leg, but they look so good. I've heard they are the most fattening fruit, and we both want to add some flesh to our bones.

At school we are teased about our weight. A boy charged at me, lunging to the ground, and then apologized: "I thought that was a long string hanging from your skirt and didn't want you to trip. But it's your leg." Everyone says Joan has more of a sense of humor than I have. She wants to taste a banana. I want it to pad my body and change what people see when they look at me.

We decide to risk Mom's rage and buy three bananas. If Mom is still in a good mood, she'll pretend she is Chiquita Banana. If not, we'll deal with the consequences.

The six blocks home are longer than the six blocks to the store. We're scared of Mom and prepare our defense: At least we bought bananas, not potato chips.

The streets are crazy with noise. Smelling the bus fumes and trash bins makes Joan gag. She's the delicate one, from the beginning marked by a scar across her neck. When she was a baby, doctors cut her tiny, pink throat to release her breath. Because she was almost a goner, Mom cherishes her. Three infants had already died, two at birth, one on the road when Mom traveled with Dad and the carnival. Joan was the seventh born, lucky seven it turned out. She lived, and deserves to be cared for.

I am the strong one, and the cold one. It's okay to scream at me. I say nasty things and keep to myself, just like my father. Sometimes they call me Mary, sometimes Little Phil, because I look just like the man from Philadelphia, originally from West Virginia, who got Sandy, our mom, pregnant four times and then left. "I don't make boys," he said when Ralph was born; he hasn't been back in two years. At first I longed for the sound of his hillbilly harmonica and tongue twisters. We weren't allowed to ask about when we would see him again, so I sought revenge by not talking for several months. "The cat got her tongue," "She has a zipper on her lips," Mom teased until I started contributing to the family chatter again. By that time I had learned a lesson I also kept forgetting: If you don't talk, you notice more.

When we get home and Mom squawks about the bananas, I do what she cannot do. I pause. Then I break my pact with Joan by inviting trouble. "If you can buy cigarettes and hair dye with the money welfare gives you to feed us, we can buy bananas with your waitress money."

Joan moves away from me toward Mom and in aggressive silence I empty the grocery bags, lovingly depositing the cherry pie in the refrigerator. So what if all hell breaks loose? Mom returns to the living room, mumbling about know-it-all snot noses who will get what's coming to them one of these days.

Having done my bad deed for the day, I say nothing when Jackie, risen from the nap she's taken after school or in place of school, burns the creamed corn. Ralph screams at the smelly funnel of smoke, frantically pumping his little fists on his highchair tray. "See what you've done now?" Mom yells at Jackie while soothing Ralph. "Ugly bastard," Jackie roars right in Ralph's face. She's the only kid in the family who is legitimate, just because her father got drunk enough to marry Mom before he split.

Mom, the shrieking peacemaker, counters, "Shut up, you little whore," and comforts Ralph while spooning toward him only the unburned portion of the corn on her plate. Joan joins Mom in feeding Ralph. "I like it burnt," she lies, keeping for herself only the charred lumps. Joan's a toady who never complains about having to feed Ralph. She is too good to be real and I am planning on being too real to be good.

Mom sits next to the playpen to watch TV and entertain Ralph. Her ninth birth was a boy, the only male she could count on staying. She would walk on hot coals for him and then swallow them, she would make all of us walk on hot coals for him, but none of us take him outside as much as we know we should. If two of us try to carry him together, he fusses, and the stroller collapses if you don't push it in exactly the right way. I feel guilty that poor Ralph is the youngest in our house of girls, most of whom never stop talking long enough to notice him, even when the TV is on, as it always is.

After dinner, I retreat to the bedroom I share with my sisters and to the single bed I share with Joan. Scrunched into a corner with a small lamp, trying not to hear the commotion in the living room, I get up once to yelp at Joan, "Homework, homework." Mom warns me to leave my sister alone. You leave me alone, I think, and then I reconfigure myself into a human desk by sitting cross-legged.

With my back up against the wall and a fortress of books in front of me, I am happy, almost. There's a slice of cherry pie and a banana in my future. When my oldest sister, Lacey, comes home I'll surprise her with a piece of pie and test her on the word *tantamount* that I had to work into a sentence for homework.

Lacey needs more vocabulary words because she says *fuck* too much. If she keeps saying it, she could lose her job at Woolworth's, where she is earning enough money to fix her teeth.

Even though we are close, I won't tell Lacey about the book I read after my homework. The library books under my bed are my secret. They take me away to a world of my own imagining where I am content, unlike Mom, who has her cross to bear. If she hadn't had all of us kids, she probably would have realized her dream: to be a famous singer.

She's singing now in the living room, so I might as well see who she is dancing with while I shake out my tingling legs. Jackie, of course, the beauty of the family, the one with green eyes that remind Mom of the emerald isle she's never visited. None of you are dogs, Mom assures us, but Jackie's got the goods. Mafia hoods in the neighborhood, guys who aspire to run numbers and beat up Puerto Ricans, are already starting to chase her because of her full head of wavy red hair and full chest. She looks much more mature than her fourteen years.

Mom's afraid Jackie will become a whore, just like our stray cat, Peaches the Whore, whose litters we mournfully drown. Jackie loves all the attention from guys and is mastering the art of flirting faster than she ever mastered any textbook. Right now I can see her practicing. That's why she and Mom are getting along tonight.

Sometimes Jackie comes home with clothing a friend outgrew, but the clothes sure look new. When she comes home reeking of cigarettes and booze, smelling familiar, like my father and her father, Mom beats her with a broom or chair, declaring she will stop only because she doesn't want to break anything. Then she turns around and soothes Jackie with a vow; she isn't one of those mothers who would throw a daughter out for getting pregnant, God forbid.

Joan and I stay up late many nights chewing on that puzzling promise. We think if Lacey gets pregnant again or Jackie gets pregnant, they should be thrown out. There's no room and Joan can't stand the stink of diapers.

It doesn't seem fair that when I'm bad, Mom threatens to send me to the foster home where she was miserable, but she would not farm out one of her pregnant daughters. Inconsistent. "My mother is inconsistent" is another sentence I stunned my teacher with. Truth is that most of the time I wouldn't mind if Jackie left, but my eyes fog with tears when I envision Lacey leaving.

Right now I want Jackie to stay. Her flirting makes the whole room crackle with laughter. She is a bonfire. I am one of those fireflies I was introduced to when the Fresh Air Fund whisked me out of our basement apartment in the Bronx to spend two summer weeks with a family in the country.

11

To make up for burning the corn, Jackie offers to cut the cherry pie, under close supervision. Each piece must be equal. We each pick up a plate and scamper out of the small kitchen, where the radiator spits and hisses at the clothing drying overhead. There's space in the living room to sit, balancing plates on our knees, or to stand and eat. Maybe people sit at tables to learn how to obey the ceremony of silverware. We all start out stabbing at the pie with a fork, but pretty soon it's a hands-on affair.

Mom grosses me out licking the red goop off Jackie's fingers, still flirting back and whispering in her ear. I disapprove, because I know it's this kind of behavior that makes you pregnant. I am never going to get pregnant, although I do like the full feeling in my belly once I have eaten my crust and Joan's discarded crust, which I use to scrape my plate clean.

I don't mind being teased about my greed and the red stain on my teeth, but I do prefer the peace of the kitchen, where I retreat to clean the plates. Wanting to keep us all together, Mom calls me back: "You went shopping, you don't have to wash up now." In my mind's eye I see the plates abandoned on the coffee table and on top of the TV. Fine food for the roaches.

I enjoy my family's company more from the other room. Once Joan gives up trying to swing her hips like Jackie, she transforms herself into a Rockette from the chorus line at Radio City Music Hall, jumping, kicking and twisting to applause. Mom claps her hands when Joan's gyrations catapult a lamp to the floor. "No damage done," she proclaims.

I wonder if she remembers the time when Dad broke a lamp. The carnival was up from the South and we were throwing a party for the whole crew. We all helped cutting and grating potatoes and cleaning up. Mom sang while frying up one batch of potato pancakes after another. Sour cream and apple sauce, beer and whiskey, popcorn and potato chips. A man we called Uncle Ray had stolen some stuffed animals from the carnival for us kids. We pranced with our bears and monkeys while Dad circled us. Mom warned him not to get carried away, which meant to slow down the drinking. When the lamp shattered, she waved a spatula at him: "I told you so, I told you so." But she was laughing. He invited her to spank him with the spatula and begged her to dance with him.

I bet she would break a lamp by throwing it at me if I went in right now and said the unthinkable: "I remember when Dad broke the lamp dancing." Even better, I could reveal myself to be a traitor worse than Judas by sighing *I miss him, I miss him,* the way I do when I rock myself to sleep with a pillow between my legs, listening for any change in Joan's snore.

I hold my tongue, mesmerized by the angry rhythm of my background music. Yet I can't thoroughly discipline the devil in me, who craves the equal piece of pie shelved for Lacey, who is a half hour late. Lacey's my hero; she is already supporting herself and doesn't have to ask Mom for anything except a place to sleep.

Balancing my foot against the bottom of the refrigerator to keep it from burping while I open the door, I abduct the plate of cherry pie and eat it in front of the bathroom mirror, safe behind the only internal locking door in the apartment. Piracy and privacy are my passions. The pie tastes stale, like guilt.

No one remembers to tell Lacey about the pie when she comes home, and she breezily rejects the banana. "Keep it for lunch tomorrow. I eat plenty at work."

At lunch the next day at school I am proud to slice a banana and arrange its rounds on top of the square of Neapolitan ice cream served on Fridays. But by Saturday I am choking on my pride. Stranded by a heavy rain, cowering under my covers late Saturday morning, I can't stop thinking about the pie I stole from Lacey.

I slog to confession solemnly prepared to tell the truth. "Forgive me, Father, for I have sinned. I ate a piece of cherry pie that belonged to my oldest sister."

He murmurs at me.

"No, you don't understand, this is serious. We hardly ever have pie."

He urges me to move on, but I persist. "This was special. We all agreed to share."

It's not fair, even my sins are ignored.

2

SLEEPWALKING
TOWARD THE HORIZON

When I bolt upright in bed, my first thought is that Mom is up to one of her old tricks: prowling around the apartment with some strange man, asking him to admire her sleeping angels, and then making noises that startle us awake.

As my eyes adjust, I spy Lacey moving around the bedroom with her bent arms in the air. She's like a mime making eerie, silent, jerky motions. Soon Joan wakes up and joins me in staring. Then Joan figures it out. "She's wrapping packages," she giggles.

That night Lacey had come home from work excited and worried about her new assignment. Supervisory responsibility over gift wrapping will mean extra cash throughout the Christmas rush. So here she is, in the middle of the night, rehearsing in her sleep for success at work. Now we understand why Lacey can come home with pretty blouses and bags of potato chips. She takes her job seriously. We will never again hog the bathroom when she's rushing for work.

Lacey is happier now that she has left school and Tommy is out of her life. High school had been hell for her. Hardly anyone had any money, but a poor white girl stood out. Shabby clothing was one thing, but the crooked buck teeth made her a billboard-size target. Welfare paid to remove teeth, but hardly ever paid for fillings and certainly never for braces. Her teeth slanted in different directions to fill the vacated spaces in her jack-o'-lantern mouth.

Lacey always smiles with her lips pursed, which wrinkles her nose in a cute way that made her boyfriend Tommy call her his bunny. He was already married, so he couldn't call her his wife. Tommy made her feel smart and beautiful at a time when Mom was dragging her down. Lacey do this, Lacey do that. The more Mom drank, the more she ordered Lacey around. She didn't notice when Lacey sobbed for hours.

In the alley outside my window one night, when Lacey was puking and groaning from the quinine Mom gave her to eject the baby, Tommy held her. Then we never saw him again. He probably doesn't even know that two months later the baby was born dead and Mom wouldn't let Lacey give it a name. Carla, Mom's best friend, agreed: "This family already has enough restless souls." I imagined unnamed pulp eternally floating in purgatory.

Sick from quinine and heartache, Lacey stopped going to high school at fifteen. The social worker, who never showed up when Lacey was truant in junior high school, quickly appeared and urged her into a job training program. Lacey eagerly chose beauty school. It was either that or secretarial training. She was much more interested in hairdos than *Dear Sirs*.

Pretty soon she sauntered home from school peacock proud, sporting a decorated beehive that could survive a tornado. "Act like you are balancing a wedding cake on your head and a good man will marry you," she happily quoted. What's on your head matters as much as what's in it if you are a woman, but Lacey wanted to master more than hair. In order to earn a higher salary, she wanted a certificate in cosmetology. But her dream didn't survive the training program, which required unaffordable supplies, so she settled for the job at Woolworth's.

Watching her show off her new hairdos reminded me of how she used to dress up and curtsey for Phil, my dad, who wasn't her real dad. No one except Mom could pick Lacey's dad out of a lineup, but she wouldn't point any fingers or name any names. She did talk about Jackie's dad, the creep. He had always been a cruel and violent drunk, but when he dangled Lacey out of a window because she wasn't his kid, Mom ditched him. At least that's what she tells us. I'm glad to have a standard for where to draw the line on the kind of abuse to take from men.

Men are the source of all happiness and all despair. Lacey knows both extremes from Phil, who left, and from Tommy, who left. She also knows that men can kill you. When she was seven she was raped on our rooftop by a neighbor who threatened to stab her to death if she ever told. She always sings that song "Up on the Roof" with a frightening dreaminess.

Lacey's best friend, Dana, would have to be lifted by a crane for anyone to dangle her out of a window. "She's not fat!" Lacey insisted in one of her rare fits of anger at us kids. Dana is always

17

nice to us, but she smells funny and wears dirty jeans and men's shirts. Her hair is short and slick with grease.

We never knew what to do when Dana paced back and forth in the courtyard waiting for Lacey to come home from work. Alice finally told her that the neighbors wondered why she prowled so much and Dana explained: "I don't like parking my car in this neighborhood." She drives all the way from Long Island to the Bronx to pick up Lacey, and then she worries about her parked car. The few times we've cruised around the city in someone's car, we've been nervous about the highway, not our neighborhood.

Dana didn't make any sense to us, but we offered to keep an eye on her Chevy for twenty-five cents an hour, half the going rate for other kinds of baby-sitting. She went for it, so we started looking forward to the nights when she arrived too early to pick up Lacey.

One night I got bored draping myself over the car with Joan and Alice, so I dashed into the house just when Lacey finally arrived. As soon as I walked into the living room, I smelled a fight. Mom was ragging on Lacey again about how a pretty girl should have a date on a Friday night and not always hang out with her best friend. She was acting like Dana wasn't even in the room; Dana was smirking. Hands on her hips, Lacey shifted her eyes and her weight until finally declaring: "Mom, Dana *is* my date. I'm a dyke now."

Mom started screaming at Dana to get the hell out of the house. Crying, she grilled Lacey: "What have I done to deserve this? Why would my first daughter become such a thing?" I stood still and stared, as if watching late-night horror movies.

Then, suddenly, another program began. Mom laughed, sort

of, and held her arms out to Lacey, who stood there looking trapped. "You know what? I don't know why I'm crying. No man ever made me happy," Mom said. "I just want my girls to be happy."

That was news to me, but Lacey seemed to believe it because pretty soon they hugged and Mom and Dana shook hands. I snuck out of the room, glad there hadn't been a fight. Lacey had told me about Dana's temper, about how she hit her once because she was wearing a skirt that was way too short.

As Lacey's fingers play the air, pleading in sign language to get it right, I want to wake her up, but I don't know what I would say.

3

PANTS AND JACKETS

In candlelight my mother's glass eye looks twice the size of her good one. She's holding the candle so close to her face that I can see the mucus that collects in the corners of her bad eye when she hasn't remembered to clean it properly. But this is not the right time to remind her. She's on a mission.

"Okay, kids, that bastard is going to turn the lights back on tomorrow!" Joan and Alice cheer, just as we usually do when Mom calls anyone or anything a bastard. If other kids mock us for not having real fathers, she assures us everyone is illegitimate in one way or another.

Mom proudly continues her announcement: "I told Aunt Carla we couldn't tolerate another night down here retreating to bed at seven P.M. It won't kill her to put us up for a short spell." I'm now cheering, too. We're getting the hell out of here.

Because I'm the oldest and tallest at home tonight, she hands me a chipped saucer with a thick candle solidly melted into it, sculpted by chance into a lopsided cupcake. Candle stumps on jar lids and in jars perch on top of dressers and on the two wardrobe closets Mom snagged at Goodwill last year. Joan and I try to ignore the scurrying, illuminated roaches as we follow Mom's expert orders. She's bossy enough to earn a reduced-rent apartment as a superintendent, but utilities aren't included.

"For Christ's sake, don't set it on fire," Mom reminds us as I hold the candle close enough for Joan to scrutinize each of the four corners of a paper bag before filling it with our clothes. We're on to the fact that roaches hide in the crevices in paper and the sleeves of sweaters. After the bag passes inspection, Joan takes the warm saucer so I can shake our clothes in the air, loosening any guests that would lead Carla to throw us out immediately.

"Don't bother with pajamas. You'll sleep in what you're wearing. Bring your schoolbooks and something to cover your ass tomorrow," Mom adds.

Tightly wrapped in plastic bags to prevent another embarrassing pest episode in school, our books are ready to go. We agree to leave our pillows behind because there's already too much stuff to carry up to street level and then up to Carla's apartment. I twirl a blanket around Ralph while teaching him the difference between "mommy" and the Egyptian "mummy" he now resembles, but he's too heavy for me to carry four flights of stairs.

A flurry of lint and dust floats in the candlelit air above us as Mom flaps and folds blanket after blanket for us to sleep on, stopping only to cluck at Ralph when he finally points to himself, clearly saying mummy, after turning to her with his mouth rounded, drawing out the word *mommy*. "See how smart you are," she coos, relieved by the recent news from a nurse who

21

declared his hearing and sight are just fine. At the clinic for some shots, Ralph was the only toddler who didn't cry or rub his arm. The nurse was kind enough to listen to Mom's questions about retardation and offer advice: "He's a quiet soul, but it wouldn't hurt to make sure someone plays with him every day no matter how busy you are."

Eager for adventure, four-year-old Alice, who was a noisy soul from the day she was born, waddles in front of Mom. Instead of carrying tomorrow's clothes, Alice has pocketed her underwear and socks, tied her sweater around her waist and, after buttoning her bulging coat, wrapped her pants around her neck like a scarf. She's twice her normal size tonight.

The flicker of candlelight alters all dimensions in our railroad apartment, which we maneuver through in single file until we arrive at the open door in the living room, where a half-moon of hallway light gels on the linoleum floor. It's a cold February night, but that room stays warm because the furnace is near our door. Everyone in the building comes down to the super's place for one thing or another and knows there's nothing to steal, so we haven't worried about locking. Mom has an open-door policy anyway. She's always willing to listen to neighbors' troubles and spill her own.

My last responsibility is to blow out every candle in the two bedrooms, kitchen and bathroom. "One of these days we'll bonfire a bon voyage to this secondhand crap, but not yet," Mom says giddily, as though sleeping someplace else for one night signals a change in our lives. She teases us. "You look like refugees, or pioneers on a wagon train in a Western." At this moment, I view everything we own and are in a new light: I think we are the most pitiful passel of pioneers ever.

Once on the street, Joan scoots ahead of Alice into the building, clutching her cargo of schoolbooks and a bursting paper bag. To amuse Alice, I pick up a ball of socks that bounces out of Joan's control. Rotating my right arm several times and loudly bubbling spit under my upper lip to imitate a propeller, I hurl the socks back at Joan, as is the right of any retriever. We play "finders keepers, losers weepers" only with things of value, like money, candy or, once, a book of cutout paper dolls from around the world that Joan found on our street.

Mom sprints up the stairs to bop me on the head, as is her right. "You're lucky those socks didn't fall through the banisters all the way downstairs." The virtue of basement living is that none of us has yet been sucked into an elevator shaft or plummeted down several flights of stairs, banging our heads on a vortex of railings. We should feel grateful that we have been spared the horrors of hallways and the dangers of the world above ground.

Usually this hallway seems dingy. Now, in contrast to our darkened apartment, the dim light reveals a world that to us appears glamorous, just as Carla's apartment appears spacious and elegant in comparison to ours. She and her son, Randy, have two bedrooms all to themselves, except on nights when her Sugar Daddy visits.

I've heard Mom say that Carla thinks she's better than everyone else just because she's been able to keep a man around for years. Then she catches herself: "The Lord should forgive my wicked tongue. Carla's had her own cross to bear."

My mom's brother, Michael, whom she hardly knew because they grew up in separate foster homes, abandoned Carla when

Randy was only two. He headed to California for a singing career, never to be heard from again, not on radio or television or through one measly phone call.

Carla has worked steadily in school cafeterias in the Bronx and Manhattan ever since, carefully harvesting gifts from a trail of married boyfriends. We've seen but never met the guy she's been with for three years or so. He's moving her and Randy into half of a house someplace you can get to only by car.

Carla's eyes well up whenever she mentions that she'll plant a garden and Randy won't have to bump his bike up four flights of stairs every night. Here on Webster Avenue, if they can't cut the locks, punks steal or slash the tires. "Out of pure malice," Carla hisses.

When our caravan files past the bike in the narrow foyer, Randy glowers and shouts: "The welfare brats have arrived." Carla rushes from the kitchen, wiping sauce on her apron and beaming at us: "It's a pajama party without pajamas." Instead of hugging any of us, she pinches her son playfully: "You behave yourself, young man, or you'll sleep downstairs and these *girls* will sleep in your room." If he doesn't behave, one of these days I will sic myself on him until I draw blood.

Carla earns her living cooking for a crowd; we'll be able to eat as much as we want. Probably not realizing there are plenty of meatballs, Joan burns her tongue by not waiting long enough for them to cool. As if the cops are at the door and she has to conceal the evidence, Alice chokes from ingesting spaghetti. Then, chugging the glass Joan hands over, her eyes widen with amazement as burning soda flows out her nose.

I can sense Carla wondering what she's gotten herself into. To calm her, I aim for perfection, but she's obliged to correct my ignorance. "That's a butter knife, girl; you only need a fork for my meatballs, and you're holding it funny."

I try to explain: "It's European."

Flustered, she turns to my mom: "What is she talking about?" Then they both ignore me.

In the cafeteria last week a new girl in school recommended that I hold my fork down instead of up. "It's not a pitchfork," she said, concentrating on each word so her British accent wouldn't interfere with her important message.

She advised me on manners in return for my instruction on the American Revolution. The class had cracked up when she pertly insisted that England granted America its freedom. Then our teacher practically shouted: "Believe me, people always have to fight for their freedom." After class, as gravely as a monk probing the Bible for guidance, I opened her textbook to the pertinent passages.

Maybe this girl will invite me to her house for dinner and I can impress her folks by using utensils the European way, but I'm better off practicing alone than in front of my family. I'd rather concentrate on eavesdropping anyway.

Tonight, Mom's gratitude short-circuits her usual objections to Carla's sensible challenges. "Jackie should not be out gallivanting at this time of night. She's only fourteen. You'd better tame her now or she'll end up like you." Later, I hear Carla prodding. "Have you made that appointment to get tied?"

Months ago I heard Carla swear "No regrets!" about having her tubes tied after her second pregnancy ended in a miscarriage. Ever since, I've imagined her perpetually twirling a knot of spaghetti in her belly. Then she lost me by grouching that men were big enough babies without her growing another one of her own: "Most of them are too impatient to put on their jackets before sliding between the sheets."

The next day I asked Lacey why boyfriends should wear jackets to bed. She responded by pinning me against the wall for an interrogation, as if suspecting me of espionage. "Who's talking to you about jackets? Has anyone touched you?"

Whenever Lacey visits, now that she is living with Dana, she pesters me about Mom's nighttime visitors, but I can't figure out what that has to do with jackets and don't dare ask another question.

Mom is answering most of Carla's questions tonight when neither one of them can squeeze out a sentence without one of us intruding. Alice itches to color, and Joan, as usual, begs to watch television before finishing her homework. Ralph, twitching and muttering, has emerged from mummification in his blanket.

Still, I overhear Mom reminding Carla that she is not responsible for Michael hitting the road. "Look, Carla, it doesn't matter what you do, men leave. You're wise to have Sugar Daddies who see you once or twice a week. You don't have to stomach someone pawing at you every night or blaming you for kids being kids. How come you're not smart enough to get over something that happened ten years ago?"

A pro at dispensing advice she can't follow, Mom confesses to anybody and everybody that she has made a mess of her life, as though she is filling out yet another welfare application. But she's proud that she graduated from a Catholic high school where she learned to speak and write better than most of our neighbors.

Every once in a while, instead of *True Romance* and *Modern Romance*, Mom reads a biography of a famous man, like the one about Adlai Stevenson she borrowed from the library. Even though she barks "show-off, show-off" at my vocabulary, she dangles such surprises as "Raising all these Childers alone is a Herculean task." When she's drunk and slurs our names, she can still pronounce her favorite big word, *lackadaisical.*

Next, I hear Carla daring to comment on the drinking. Mom stalls by reacting to Ralph's cry. Carrying him back to the couch where Carla waits, she gushes: "I so appreciate a night of adult conversation. I can't thank you enough for taking us in."

Carla, I can't thank you enough, either. For the meatballs and the eavesdropping, for the feast of secrets you two usually hoard.

Last summer, they disappeared together too many nights. Carla would sing in the doorway, "Sandy, it's time for walking and whining," and Mom would drop everything. She'd turn off the stove if she was boiling macaroni water or heating beans and leave me simmering with resentment about watching Ralph and Alice.

Sometimes when Mom goes out, we don't see her again until the next morning. It's always a bad sign when she struts around the house in a black slip while applying makeup. "I'm just going out for an hour. I'll be right back with dinner," she lies, looking me right in the face.

Joan sometimes moans, "Where are you going?" which makes Mom snap, "I'm going crazy, wanna come?" With black chevrons thickly penciled around her eyes and her lips painted red, she already looks crazy to me.

If several hours pass and the kids spin out of control, I

occasionally force Joan to trudge upstairs to ask Carla for help locating Mom. Carla always acts disturbed: "What, she's not home yet?" Joan reports that one night Carla cursed. If she's not too tired from work, she'll ask if we've eaten yet and force Randy to bring down some food, which he delivers with an insult and a smile. "Charity for the scavengers; leftovers for the leeches." No one can convince me and Joan he's just teasing or that only sticks and stones hurt.

Jackie has warned us that once Carla moves, we're going to be up shit's creek. Not that Jackie will help any. She doesn't go to school and she hardly ever comes home before midnight. When she is home, she's either sleeping or curling her hair. Walking in the door, I can detect her presence from the smell of perfume and burnt hair.

Joan and I realize we're on our own. In an emergency a neighbor lets us use her phone, when it's connected. If we beg, Lacey hops the train all the way from Queens, no matter how late it is or how early she's due at work. I try to play it cool when Dana picks up. One time she screamed, "You're an endless pit, you know that?" before slamming down the phone. I had been sniveling that we had not seen Mom in a whole day, there was no food, Alice was sitting under the kitchen table banging pots and pans, and Ralph was eating paint chips off the wall. I know better than to cry my heart out most of the time. Inside there's a steady, quiet moan: *I want to go to school. If I miss classes, I'll end up left back like Jackie and Lacey. I like the school lunch! I want. I want. I want my goddamned mother to come home.*

Some nights I leave Joan alone to watch the kids while I stalk the bars. Others, Joan and Alice come with me, leaving Ralph sleeping in the crib. If we are lucky, Mom's at the first bar; if not, we troop to all three of her places. If our mission is doomed, she's not at any of them and none of her friends drops a clue. "Your mother has to have a life," or "Sandy deserves a little time off," they chide. We didn't ask to be born, so they shouldn't treat us like trespassers on our mother's life.

Before entering a bar, I pout in the doorway, aiming to suction Mom out of the smoky haze. Most of the regulars who stare back consider me a cutie and a sad sack, an annoyance and a godsend. Drunks can't keep themselves from dripping their intoxicated thoughts on you.

Sometimes Mom lets me lead her home. If she's cuddling with someone, he may hand me hurry-up-and-go money when I whisper that the kids are hungry.

I dread and depend on the creeps who razz contributions from cronies by waving a dollar at me for a slow dance. They smell like ashtrays, shit and whiskey. Instead of gracefully holding my shoulders and head straight the way Arthur Murray dance studio commercials advise, I arch my back so none of the gorillas can rest their paws on my butt. Transformed into a four-legged creature, I'm poised to bolt from captivity in the unnatural human world. Four bucks and I'm out of there.

If it's one of Rico's nights at the bodega, he swiftly bags more than could be bought at the grocery store, including Joan's favorite, Dinty Moore Beef Stew. Even though Jackie calls the bodega "the dirty spic store," I prefer it to her hangout, the Italian place where they run numbers and there's no orange juice.

"Look at the expire dates," Rico encourages me, pointing to a small glass refrigerator. A container of milk or orange juice stamped with the current day is mine. Sometimes the milk is sour because the refrigerator isn't always cold enough, but usually it's good. If I net both, I dart between Alice and her appetite. She forgets that combining milk and orange juice makes her puke.

I hate it when Mom stays out all night, and I'm repelled by her coming home late with a man in tow. I spied on her in the living room only once. That's when I figured out the expression "mooned." While she sat on the sofa, a man with his shirt on but his pants off stood in front of her gurgling and sighing. His butt glowed in the dark, swaying like a lantern. Then he lost balance and had to lean on the arm of the couch.

I guess I don't want all my questions answered, because I ran back to bed praying that Joan would not wake up, gasping for breath, after I pulled the covers over our heads.

Now when Mom springs open the convertible couch in the living room for company, I climb on top of a dresser and reach for the water pipes overhead. I swing to the rhythm of the creaking mattress. My hands are dried and hardened from blisters, like my dad's when he was a day laborer hauling boxes out of trucks until some union guys cleaned his clock. If I yell at Mom that it's more important for me to attend school than to take care of Alice and Ralph when she has a hangover, she gripes that I'm callous. I wish that my heart was more like my hands.

It's Lacey who noticed my leathery hands. After I explained, she pulled me down on the floor and hugged me so I wouldn't see her eyes moisten. "You know what, Mom's always with drunks. They take too long to finish their business." Revving herself up to emit more truth, she loosened her hold on me and drummed the linoleum with one fist. "I'm sorry you have to listen to this garbage. I'm sorry you have to grow up so fast, but the kids need you too much for me and Dana to take you in. We would, you know. I love you, punk."

It's too bad dykes can't have babies, because Lacey would make the best mother. Like her, I'll find work as soon as I can and I'm never going to be a mother. I only intend to play aunt for Joan, Alice and Ralph, keeping my distance while I help out. If I start hugging the kids, I'm afraid I'll never stop crying.

4

TRIUMPH AND SHAME

Mom nagged Lacey to visit tonight mostly to goad her into taking a swing at Jackie. Mom used to discipline Jackie herself, grabbing any handy item she could find. One time Jackie was rushed to the emergency room after the dustpan caught the corner of her eye; after that, she accused Mom of wishing all her kids had only one eye. Now that Jackie is so strong, she intimidates Mom. She'll wheel around at the slightest threat, her voice booming with authority as if she were the parent. "Don't you dare, or you'll regret it."

Lacey is older and stronger than Jackie, especially now that she's experimenting with alternative consciousness and popping pills that make her pace like a lion. Jackie doesn't need drugs to prowl and pounce; she has always threatened us with flash floods of anger. I can be in the middle of a conversation with her, once again trying to explain how we live in the twentieth century even if it is 1963, and suddenly she becomes hostile, as if in combat against the reason she's been left back twice and still lacks the patience, ability or hope to learn the basics.

Mom's beef is that Jackie is mixed up with the wrong people. "You don't get clothes and jewelry just for being pretty," she smirks. "That guy is Bad News, you hear me?" Jackie flounces her hair, waving away Mom's criticism.

Mom is consistently inconsistent. When Bad News first came around, she flirted with him, coyly offering coffee or tea as if she were a stewardess. He figured out that something sure as shit was expected from him in exchange for dating her jailbait daughter. On his way out the door two weeks ago, he looped an arm around Jackie's neck in an affectionate stranglehold, pulling her in close, showing off. Then he whipped out forty bucks for Mom, telling her to do something nice for the kids.

Mom looked like a kid herself as she walked toward him, her head down, and accepted the money. "Say thank you," he sneered. She said nothing.

The next time he came around, he swaggered while draping brand-new dresses for Mom, me, Alice and Joan all over the couch. The sizes were perfect. Then he hustled to his car and reappeared with a box for Ralph, growling: "He needs some boy toys."

It felt like Christmas, except Mom was stringing insults instead of lights. "That stuff cost him nothing. It comes right out of his father's warehouse on Jerome Avenue. Stolen goods."

I don't care where my three new dresses came from as long as they weren't stolen from anyone in my class. As the only non-Jew and the only welfare kid in the highest-track classes, I already stand out too much, thanks to my fourth-grade teacher last year, who Joan is stuck with this year. This lady tormented me by telling the entire class I got an F in Hygiene for crud under my nails and no proof of dental and eye exams in my files. Now two of the boys call me Cruddy Childers and mock me because on Jewish holidays I'm the only one at my desk "when I could be home cleaning my nails."

Another day she made me an example for the whole class, excusing me from assembly for wearing a blouse that looked gray next to everyone else's sparkling clean white shirts and blouses. She waited years to direct Honors Four and wasn't about to let a welfare kid ruin it. A few kids protested, "That's not fair," and when I flipped the bird, they clapped.

My teacher gained fury like a storm. "Leave my room!" She released a poison arrow from deep in her throat. "To the principal's office. You're disrupting my class again."

"The principal is your pal" is the saying that helps me remember how not to confuse the head of school with a principle, meaning an idea that has virtue, so I sputtered at him, "She picks on me constantly. The other kids will back me up."

While sorting through a pile of papers, the principal offered me gum and sympathetic glances. I didn't break down and cry until he said: "I believe you." He escorted me back to class and in front of everyone lectured my teacher. "Children get into this class on the basis of their reading and math scores. She belongs here more than you do, apparently."

I could tell she knew she had crossed the line. But winning isn't all it's cracked up to be. A brew of triumph and shame contaminated my concentration for days after that. I'd glare at her, remembering how she suspended the black girl who punched

Andrew, the class pet. After that black girl was kicked out of our class, I glimpsed her only once. I said hi as I approached, but she pushed me. "I'm in the class with all the black kids now, where I belong," she shouted. "You'd better watch where you end up!" I said nothing, fractured by sadness for her and fear that she'd prey on me.

This year is much better at school. My fifth-grade teacher must have heard that the principal is on my side, because she is extra nice to me. When she realized I couldn't afford the class trip or milk and cookies, she paid me to alphabetize her travel folders. Aruba, Bahamas, Bermuda, California, Denmark: she's dreaming of traveling all over the world after she gets married. Growing up in Iowa, she always knew she belonged elsewhere, she tells the whole class. The best teachers never stay for long, but for Joan's sake I'm hoping this one will stick around at least another year.

When kids giggled at the poem I wrote about white snow in the city turning brown from soot and dog shit, she hushed them. "The assignment was to write a poem about something you actually saw, not something you think you are supposed to see. You're not writing Hallmark greeting cards." She didn't even grade me down for cursing. I had tried *poop*, but it didn't yield a rhyme as perfect as *dog shit* and *city grit* for the closing two lines.

This teacher doesn't expect me or anyone else to lie, and probably would disapprove if she knew I wore stolen goods. But I'm not a thief, and there's no point in letting clothes fade away in warehouses. Even my teacher had criticized the government for bribing farmers to let wheat rot in barns rather than distributing it to starving people in poor countries.

Tonight Mom booms accusations about Jackie stealing from

her purse and from the refrigerator, which is missing a six-pack. "She's a slut who treats the house as if it is her very own flophouse, just like her father did." Mom raves, as drunk on booze as Lacey is high on her stuff. "She stole my brown heels and broke them. The only decent pair of heels I own."

"Leave, Jackie, leave," I plead wordlessly, but she lashes out.

"You old hag. You're angry that no one wants you and your sagging tits anymore. Even your hair is falling—"

Jackie hits the ground before finishing her sentence. Lacey has lunged into action. "Never talk to Mom that way, you hear me, whore?"

Jackie knows she can't win, but the devil in her is a fighter who dreads disgrace more than fists. Weasel-watching from behind the couch, I pray one of the neighbors will hear the screaming and call the cops. Before it's too late, oh please, before it's too late.

After she pins Jackie on the floor, Lacey grabs the broken shoe from Mom. First she ineffectually pounds, then she scrapes Jackie's stockings off her legs with the heel, which has a nail jutting out of it. Soon the spike lodges in Jackie's calf, and blood spurts.

I want to bellow, "Stop, Lacey, stop, she's going to bleed to death," but I say nothing; I'm too slow to duck a curse, a fist or a flying shoe.

Lacey stops anyway, as soon as Jackie crumbles, sobbing about scars.

During the fight, Alice and Joan trembled in the doorway, covering and uncovering their eyes, ready to run. When Lacey slumps away, they rush to shield Jackie's body with their own, as if protection is better late than never.

Lacey has won again, but I can see she feels more shame than triumph. The last time this happened, she stormed out of the apartment, threatening never to come back. "Mom, you have to stop pitting Jackie and me against each other like we're roosters." Later she told me Mom couldn't help it, she must have learned to favor fighting at the orphanage, like a James Cagney character.

5

CONEY ISLAND

Mom is talking so fast, Joan and I can't grasp the details, but we know it's Good News. Someone who knows someone owes Jackie's boyfriend big time, so his crew will paint our apartment for free. They will even move and cover the furniture. Best of all, each room will bloom in a different color.

Surprising us with four brushes and a boxed tray of paints, Mom offers us a bonus for being such good kids. "It won't break my back to move the dressers away from the wall in your bedroom today. This way, you guys can paint one wall any way you want until the professionals arrive."

The notion of professional painters working in our house inspires Mom to organize us. She assigns the wall space closest to the floor to Ralph, sweeps her arms across the stretch of canvas Alice can reach, and invites me and Joan to decorate the rest of the wall "with our dreams." Climbing on chairs and dressers to reach higher and higher is permitted; painting with someone directly below forbidden. Joan and I cross our hearts and swear to keep an eagle eye on Ralph. Otherwise, he'll poison himself licking a brush full of paint.

Mom twinkles her good eye at us. Her new boyfriend, Wally, doesn't have much to say for himself, but instead of being one of those creeps who treats kids like clunky furniture, he respects her resolve to be a good mother. The weekend the painters come he'll spring for an outing. When I'm told he's worried about us breathing in fresh paint, especially in an apartment with minimal ventilation, I wonder what he expects from us.

Mom recites her plan. "If the weekend is good the Saturday the crew comes, we're off to Coney Island even though it's too early to swim. All of us, Lacey, too. Every year we should take a trip, even if it's just a picnic in Crotona Park."

If she's excited about something in the future, Mom creates new rules left and right. The other night she crammed all of us around the kitchen table for supper: "No elbows, you hear." When she broke the rule first, we chanted: "Mabel, Mabel, if you're able, get your elbows off the table."

Because of the color she usually dyes her hair, everyone calls Mom Sandy, but her real name is Mabel, which turns out to be convenient sometimes. Around Thanksgiving, she introduces herself as Mabel to the Baptists who distribute free turkeys and baskets of fixings with bows and prayer cards on the handles. Old-fashioned names go over well with do-gooders.

We're all confused about names. My dad's name is Donald, but everyone called him Phil. Mom never married him, but she and the rest of us, including the ones who aren't his, claim his last name. To jeer at him jilting us, Mom insists on pronouncing the name *Child*-ers, even though Dad pronounced it *Chill*-ders. After a neighbor informed us that officially Jackie and Lacey are only half-sisters of the rest of us, Mom referred to her as Nosey Rosie. What counts, Mom winks, is the Mabel label. We are sisters, plain and simple.

One strictly enforced rule of the house is that we cannot utter Lacey's given name, Adele. Just hearing it galls Mom; she fumes about Lacey's father choosing that name and then not sticking around to ever hear his kid talk. To top it all off, when Mom's drunk, she can't keep our names straight, so she uses numbers. When I try to fetch her from Rudy's, Pete's, or the Bronx Cheer, her hangouts, she introduces me as number three. Jackie has it worse, because she's number two, as in "There's no toilet paper and I have to go number two."

When Alice practically foams at the mouth begging to trot beside me on a mission to track down Mom and a meal, she becomes the center of attention for being number 5. That's the point when everyone comments on the size of Sandy's family.

If she's a sad-sack drunk, Mom discloses to anyone who will listen that these are the numbers for the kids who are still alive. When she recalculates, I'm number six. The God-given numbers one, three and four were stolen from her early. People look at me as if I'm blessed for having escaped the wrath of God.

I don't want them to know that traveling in a filthy carnival with my father killed Mom's first son. Since I wasn't born yet, I don't acknowledge him as my brother any more than I mourn Jackie's stillborn twin as my lost sister. Mom claims that Jackie's father's beatings during her pregnancy killed the twin and, reaching into the womb, christened Jackie as a fighter. Secretly, she probably feels guilty that, outside the womb, she nurtured Jackie's fighting spirit by beating her to get even with her father. Putting the finishing touches on the tragedies associated with her one and only official husband, Mom often adds that her second pregnancy with "that certifiable madman" ended in a crib death.

"What a tragedy. Nothing prepares you for crib death," people murmur. The same people might exclaim, "What a crime," if they knew that when Mom vanishes for a day Ralph spends hours in his crib or playpen whimpering or wailing as if he's about to die.

If Mom is a happy drunk, she shrugs off comments about all the Childers children: "I'm an Irish-Catholic girl." That's another name that perplexes me. Being Irish-Catholic explains not using birth control, but it's supposed to also mean you don't have illegitimate children. People classify themselves as Irish-Catholic, Italian, Puerto Rican, Negro or black, Haitian, and Jewish, but I don't stamp myself as anything, except maybe a girl from the Bronx. St. Patty's Day signifies little to me except that it's the day Mom can be counted on to scrounge up enough money for corned beef and cabbage and to imitate a brogue when she refers to us as a crew of hungry micks.

Being Catholic mostly means that I consider myself an explorer of the territories designated *a state of sin* and *a state of grace*. When seized by uncharitable thoughts, such as "He's ugly" or "She's a bitch," I'm in a state of sin. I was a sinner when I stroked Ralph's weenie to calm him down the two times I was stuck taking care of him most of a Saturday. When he curled and glowed like one of those blissful, fat naked angels you see on Christmas cards, I felt justified. But shadow thoughts loomed

41

over the crib when for the second time I reached for his nub of pink flesh. It's not right to satisfy my impatience and curiosity this way. It feels like I'm seeking revenge, even though I don't want to harm Ralph. Maybe this is what causes crib death? Resentment is a state of sin that leads me to steal happiness from Ralph and Alice by taking dangerous shortcuts when I'm forced to baby-sit. I won't do it again.

Although the priests used to say we have to cultivate a sinless existence to reap a state of grace, that's not how I see it. I can sin one day and wake up in a state of grace the next. I worship the beauty of small things, like morning light, Alice's skin and a perfect line in a Robert Frost poem that I remember all day without even trying, as if I've found an eternal peppermint. Problem is, as soon as you share peppermints, you don't own them anymore. To avoid the sin of selfishness it is necessary to sacrifice a state of grace. That's why attending Mass is stupid; seeing all those people ruins any state of grace that arrives with the morning.

The name I do understand, even if I'm not sure about pronunciation, is Childers. No matter what, we have an obligation to conduct ourselves as a family. Intermittently Mom reminds us of the rules of the tribe. You can fight like cats and dogs with each other, but you'd better beat the shit out of any outsider who tries to lay a hand on one of your own. Family always makes room for you at the table, even if there isn't enough food to go around; only a relative will smile when saying, "You eat, I ate yesterday." Family is fate; no one will ever love you as much. Among ourselves, my sisters whisper that we owe Mom because she could have deserted us just like her mother left her and her brother. No matter how energetically we jostle each other in our small space, like agitated molecules, we remember that family shields us from the world, which is a perilous place for girls and for poor people. Most of the time I tell myself that my family feels like a lifeline, not a prison sentence, but I always have one eye on the door.

Being a member of the family means I must praise the kids for painting their portion of the wall and share the excitement when we realize that Ralph's two-and-a-half-year-old hands are strong and steady enough for him to draw outlines of animals from books.

"He's a genius," Mom declares, summoning neighbors who nod that yes, the kid can draw. Maybe he can draw because we give him little opportunity to talk. His halting speech and red face when no one listens distinguish him from the rest of us. We all talk at the same time, contributing to the flurry of stories and complaints that threaten to drown out communication whenever more than two people are in a room. We're sparrows twittering in a picked-over tree, anxiously awaiting the arrival of the next storm. Our chatter overwhelms Ralph, who usually disregards our dutiful "How's our little boy?" It's only with his miniature paintbrush that somehow he knows how to swirl, communicate and hear our praise.

Frustrated that we can't control the paint drip, Joan and I switch to thick charcoal pencils. Soon half of our bedroom wall is shadowed with trees and mountains copied from some of the duplicate travel brochures I lifted from my teacher. Until they were splattered with paint, I planned on returning them.

Every day after school for a week, Joan and I approach the wall, our arms aching from holding them up so long, while Ralph lies on his side pushing a brush until a figure resembling an animal emerges. But the thrill dwindles and Joan and I tire of banging into the misplaced mountains of dressers and chairs crowded in the middle of the room. We're relieved on the day the painters arrive to cover our messy masterpiece with what Mom identifies as quality paint and professional technique. There's some suspense about the colors that will appear on our walls while we are out, but mostly we're wondering if our luck will hold long enough to deliver Coney Island weather.

On Saturday morning Mom's boyfriend, Wally, leaves early, as he always does, and there are no beer bottles in sight. Mom starts singing to awaken Alice and Joan. "Let's get an early start, kids. It'll be warm enough for a crowd."

Alice sits up dazed just like it was any old morning, rolling and scratching her neck like a cat when Mom sits on her pillow so that she can brush her hair. Wally surprised us with a big bottle of something called cream rinse that prevents tangling and knotting. Now fixing her hair doesn't wring tears out of Alice. Joan is starting to grab the brush more, although she still refuses to scrub her face in the morning.

Mom guessed right; the train is mobbed. "If Dana was a decent sort, she would have let Lacey drive us instead of sticking us in a cattle car," she gripes, but then corrects herself, maybe realizing it was mean to exclude Lacey's girlfriend from the outing. "No complaining today, kids, you hear? We're gonna have the kind of time you'll remember. I don't want you grumbling to your own kids about an unhappy childhood, at least not while I'm still around. We should be grateful for what we have."

At the second stop on the train, we are indeed grateful. Because of the departure of a sprawling man, Mom could sit down with Ralph in her lap and Joan and Alice on each side. They scrambled for the seats before anyone else, leaving me safeguarding the cooler, the folded stroller, and a huge duffel bag until I could drag my cargo over, careful to avoid bumping the other people forced to stand.

Today Mom accepts the fact that both Lacey and Jackie had other things to do. Having warned Jackie that there would be hell to pay if she stood us up, she still isn't upset that Jackie didn't come home last night or this morning. "Jackie knows full well I can't lug all of you and this stuff myself. I guess she has other fish to fry." Mom must be in a state of grace, because she's tracking the silver lining: "Maybe he'll marry her and take her off my hands. Then you girls can have your own beds."

She can't say much more on the train because we can hardly hear each other over the radios blasting Spanish music, babies crying and the grinding and screeching of the train wheels. Besides, we have to use our eyes more than our mouths. Once we missed our station and had to endure four more stops for a free transfer back. Even if Wally forked over enough money for extra tokens, we wouldn't want to carry all this crap up and down stairs to switch directions.

I'm the one standing, so I'm the scout. At the stop before ours, I'll start moving everything toward the door so that we can beat other people heading to Brooklyn. The ride on the next train is a long journey if you're seated, a trial if not.

Scanning the scene by pretending to check out people's shoes, I'm puzzled by the two Puerto Rican boys standing at the head of the car. Do they have knives in their pockets? They are certainly throwing dagger-like glances at the black guy slouched over two seats who is staring back at them as if he's ready for anything. Casual posture is sometimes a sign of being strung out, but this guy is as alert as I am trying to be. Carrying yourself casual also declares that you're at home everywhere; he owns the train. I don't like the looks of the two Irish boys staking claim to the middle of the car, either. They're probably brothers, maybe off-duty cops, maybe hoodlums pretending to protect others.

When the elevated train dips underground and speeds into unknown neighborhoods, we're nervous each time the train door rattles open. There's a possibility thugs will board to amuse themselves by terrorizing people, even in broad daylight. We've heard so many reports of subway crime, we're anticipating our turn.

Virtually every family on the train designates a hawk to detect the danger zones where action might flare. Mothers and older sisters tuck their heads down and keep kids close, listening. If we hear any of these guys calling each other out, the wise ones won't linger to see who is bluffing. It's best to flee before the knives fly. Everyone knows what happens if you interfere with teenage boys proving their manhood. This is how easily cowards are born: it takes only one tale of the critical physical condition of someone who tried to make peace. We're neither heroes nor witnesses; we're just trying to survive.

Our luck holds. We transfer before any of the guys makes a move. The next train arrives quickly and with room for everyone. After Memorial Day, the train will turn into a moving zoo with collective voices roaring that the city should run extra cages to the beaches on summer weekends.

Once on the beach, Mom deliberates, her head as clear as the sky today. We'll spread our blankets and towels close to the water, in a direct line from the concessions, at a decent distance from other pockets of people. Then she confesses the Bad News. "Wally stiffed me. Men don't know what it takes to feed growing girls and a boy." We'll each wolf two PB&J sandwiches made with the squashed loaf of bread and two jars in the duffel bag. One ice cream or cotton candy each now or later; before the return trip we'll split hot dogs and sodas. "No sniveling about being hungry or wanting candy. Just think about all those poor kids in China who eat nothing but rice day after day." To quench our thirst, Joan and I will traipse back and forth to the concession area to fill the thermos with cold water. We're not complaining. I'll be happy as long as Mom doesn't buy beer or, even worse, flirt one out of an innocent bystander.

We shriek when the shock waves of freezing water first hit our bellies. Ralph screams only once, his nostrils burning from saltwater. Until Mom's arms tire, she swings his legs back and forth into the water, his laughter dipping and rising with her. Otherwise, we take turns tending him. Alice splashes with him in the shallow water, threatening to kiss him with the purplish lips that testify to how long she jumped up to her waist in the frigid mini-waves close to shore.

Although no one would stoop to steal our dinky radio or ripped towels, I welcome my turn to guard our stuff. Reading on the beach without any of the kids bothering me is one of the most peaceful events in my life. Still, to entertain Alice and Ralph, I've promised to underline goofy paragraphs in *Gulliver's Travels*.

After we dry off, lather each other with baby oil and nap, Mom grows reckless, even though she hasn't chugged any beer: "Let's throw out these rags so we don't have to carry them all night. I'll order brand-new towels from Lenny."

I know as well as she does about Lenny's excessive charges. He pops up with each welfare check, demanding payment for blankets that began pilling after the second wash; they have more lint than wool in them. I'm afraid Mom is starting to count on Wally to bail her out, as if each kiss is money in the bank.

While struggling to steer Ralph's crippled stroller through the crowd to the rides, Mom envelops me with her arms and a conspiratorial whisper. "We're all riding the Cyclone together. The ticket collector isn't supposed to do it, but he'll watch our stuff."

Mom, Ralph and Alice climb into one car of the roller coaster, and Joan and I settle in front of them. Mom screams and laughs louder than anyone, until suddenly she's yelling: "Oh shit, my glasses." To cheers behind us, Joan's arm shoots up and catches Mom's glasses swooping in the air. As her arm lurches back down, slamming her hand and the glasses on the crossbar, one lens pops out and flies away.

Oh boy, wait until Mom sees this. She'll lose her temper. The day will be ruined. I'm usually anxious for the clanging finale of a roller coaster ride, yet at the same time I long for it to last. My quandary is worse than ever this time. Mom believes Joan saved her glasses, and Joan and I dread admitting the truth. Joan squeezes back her tears as she rubs her hand with pain and worry.

"Hey," Mom surprises us after the ride, "we're not heading for a funeral. Cheer up. You lost the lens on my left side. They haven't yet invented a formula to make a glass eye see."

48

It's a little chilly when we head back to the station, but there was so much sun today all moods are elevated. Strangers entertain each other's babies and smile while helping to lift strollers. On the train ride home, we nod out, Ralph spread across Mom's and Joan's laps, our heads flopping on one another's shoulders like a row of mops in a cartoon.

"Looking forward to crawling into bed?" Mom prompts all of us, including Ralph, to drone with the train: "There's no place like home; there's no place like home."

6

MOVING

Now we know why Mom didn't blow up about losing a lens. I observed her dramatically poke through the empty frame to her immobile glass eye, intending to entertain Wally the Wallet. "I look cockeyed instead of like a cocktease!" Then she switched tactics. In a monotone, she prophesied hours of waving an application for new glasses while on long lines at the welfare office.

"Of course, the frames they distribute are out of style, so be it," she told him, as if nothing important was being discussed. He remained utterly silent, even when Mom repeated herself three times, her nervous voice accelerating toward desperation.

Finally, Wally stood up, pulled out a bill and plopped down again. Climbing on his lap, hugging and kissing him, Sandy aimed to convince Santa she was a good girl, until his pronouncement propelled her back into her own seat. "Sandy, this is the last time. I can't keep up with you. You must think I'm made of gold. There's my own kids, you know."

Begging often boomerangs: Wally zinged into reverse motion out of our lives. He wasn't anything to look at, a runt, really. But he didn't drink much and was gentle, probably exhausted from working two jobs. They didn't even have sex every night he came over; they just peacefully spooned.

Mom refuses to pine. "No matter what I did, I couldn't make the man laugh. Besides, I have much bigger things to worry about, so you kids better behave yourselves," she warns us one night before heading out. The end of Wally spells the return of drinking. She's making up for lost time, just like when she renounced cigarettes for Lent and then smoked two packs the day it was over.

Mom is right, though. Wally is the least of our problems. Suddenly, yellow demolition notices flap on windows and caravans of U-Hauls crawl and honk through our narrow streets. The news is shocking. Our row of four-story buildings has been condemned. There's no cross ventilation and kids are inhaling too much smoke and roach spray.

"Mom has known for months," Lacey confides. "She counted on Wally to pitch in."

We're assured by our social worker that once the projects around the corner are finished, we'll top the list for a brand-new three-bedroom. Joan drags him through our apartment, pointing out the cream, lavender and peach walls, but he won't promise that each room can be painted a different color in the projects.

Mom contacts a few agencies to find another job as a super, but it turns out that women only manage the types of tenements slated for destruction all over the city, to be replaced by a highway or public housing. Mom throws her hands up in the air: "The welfare pittance covers only a one-bedroom in a neighborhood where whites aren't outnumbered." She stomps: "There's no point in moving if it's to another slum or to projects."

Only drinking muffles her worries as eviction day looms. But I have no way to avoid fretting, although digging pins into my cuticles calms me a bit. "Mom," I nag, "you have to keep looking."

I'm dismissed with "Easier said than done," as if talking about it makes the problem worse.

Instead of packing on Doomsday, we frantically wait for the bulldozer. That day ends with Mom's triumphant cackling. "The city never does anything on time." But soon we are informed that the wreckers will definitely cart all of our belongings out to the curb in five weeks.

When sober, Mom suffers from headaches and heartaches. In response to questions about where we are going, she whips out her old standby: "We're going crazy." She rants and raves about the cost of apartments and the nerve of landlords in decent neighborhoods. They don't want to rent to people on welfare or harbor five kids and one adult in a one- or two-bedroom apartment. She bellows that she can't take it anymore. Why she kept us this long when she can do so little for us is one of god's mysteries. Maybe we would all be better off in an orphanage or foster home, if only we could be housed together. When one of us annoys her, she shoves clothes into a few paper bags, unfolds a couple of bucks, and fiercely orders the miscreant to sit outside until the cab to the orphanage arrives. We spend the taxi money on candy before creeping back downstairs, where she greets us with contrite kisses, as if regretting sending us on an unfair shopping errand. We all know that she won't actually dump us the way her mother dumped her, but some nights the drums of anxiety fiercely beat in our hearts, threatening separation, separation, separation.

Jackie, Joan and Alice, convinced she is searching as much as possible, cheer her on to success. "You're the best, Mom." I can't join the chorus, even though I do feel guilty that we ruined her life. "Give Mom more credit," Jackie commands. "She's wearing herself out inspecting rat-infested shit holes."

When a social worker comes by once again to warn the hangers-on about the eviction, he seems pleased to have located a three-bedroom for us in a project in Harlem. "Get out of here," Mom screams, threatening him with the same rusted cast-iron frying pan she once threw at Dad. "You can't send a white family of girls into that jungle. It'll be on your head if my girls are raped."

I'd rather doubt my mother than believe that there is no place for us to live. But the newspapers I steal verify her complaints: most of the listings are scams or require agent fees. People locate apartments through friends. Finally one of our remaining neighbors tips us on how she found a place with clean halls and huge rooms in a West Bronx neighborhood about twenty blocks away. To avoid inquiries from colored people and the cost of advertising, landlords post "For Rent" signs in windows. All you have to do is ring the super's bell. I salvage the map she drew for Mom from the trash and vow to head to the West Bronx the following Saturday.

Tackling the stone steps leading up the hill from our street two at a time, catching my breath on every other landing by turning around to gaze at how far I've come, I'm perplexed. From a distant height, Webster Avenue looks quaint rather than dingy. I agree with Mom; it doesn't seem right that these four-story brick buildings hugging one another will be torn down instead of repaired. But I'm willing to move to the cleaner streets the lady described as winding all the way to the Harlem River, which separates the Bronx from Manhattan.

Legs aching from the stairs, I stretch them running down the hill that slopes past my school, leading to a street that then reaches up to a wide avenue. This must be the Grand Concourse etched in two thick lines on the map. A necklace of little parks with benches bisects the avenue. On both sides, tall buildings with bay windows, patios, ornamental sculptures and fanciful decorations resembling cake frosting pose for my amazed eyes. There's no litter on the ground or graffiti on the benches. I can't believe there's such a beautiful place this close to where I live and no one told me about it.

Once I tramp down the hill on the other side of the grand avenue, I'm dumbfounded. Maps lie just like people, and my hopes rise and fall like hills. I expected to find streets named University and Ogden where apartments were supposedly available, but instead I confront a maze of unmarked blocks snaking at angles from Jerome Avenue to the Edward L. Grant Highway. The map indicates neither the highway nor the steep set of stairs hulking on the other side. I have arrived at Nowhere Avenue. Instead of parking my butt on an unfamiliar stoop flanked by a pawnshop and a dark, narrow candy store, I retreat, ashamed of abandoning my quest and letting down my family.

When I get home, Mom has no time to listen to details; she

just warns me not to make her feel bad that we can't live where I choose. But then suddenly she is including me in her plans. "It's no wonder you didn't make it across town on those skinny legs. We'll check out those streets together." It turns out the neighbor lady left behind some landlords' phone numbers, and Mom had spent the morning at the pay phone on the corner scribbling appointments and directions. We'll take a bus over the highway and hoof it five blocks beyond the last stop. If I scuttle behind Mom with my head down and the bus is nearly empty, no half-human bus driver will enforce the motto "Little enough to ride for free, little enough to ride your knee."

After we visit the third apartment, Mom croons that I am her good luck charm. My politeness and her good looks influenced the landlord's verdict. "Even though you are on welfare, you can have the apartment. All of my tribe is moving to Yonkers and Forest Hills." Little did he know the size of our tribe, but we figured he wouldn't throw us out once we moved in.

Two weeks later we climb out of our condemned basement lair into a first-floor apartment with windows in four rooms. Mom brags, "Living adjacent to the courtyard suits us. Before we know it, we'll snare a penthouse." She overflows with delight, reminding us there are happy endings: "We now have the good fortune to reside on Shakespeare Avenue."

Close by there is a triangular park with benches and trees across from a library built of gray stone and genuine marble. On the way to the park, a wide sidewalk in front of the Church of the Sacred Heart provides a stage for all the christenings, weddings, funerals and regular Masses. Parades of fancy dresses and suits come and go several days a week. Gleaming limousines line up along our block, reflecting back the sun. The church opens its doors at five-thirty A.M. and closes around ten P.M.; when it's vacant I can trick myself into a trance by staring at the stained glass and wood carvings of the Stations of the Cross. But I won't be tricked into believing in God. I've decided I'm like Paula, the Jewish girl I met the first day we moved in. To advertise our agnosticism, we roller-skate together around the statue of the Virgin Mary until the nuns descend from the third-floor convent, pointing fingers and blowing whistles, summoning God's punishment and our laughter.

My street is almost as fine as the Grand Concourse, where Paula tells me rich people live in doorman buildings. Chills rake through me when an old man with a brogue, gesturing at the steep hill behind us, identifies our neighborhood as a distant cousin of the Appalachian Mountains farther south. The small of my back and my throat tickle with recognition that I am descended from hill dwellers. After all, my father is called hillbilly Phil because his twang came from the West Virginia hills he had lived in as a boy before his mother, seeking work, dragged her kids to the city. That is about all I know of his boyhood; it is enough for me to be convinced that if he wanted to, he could track us down here.

Running up the hills and across a park at the high point near my new school, I push myself harder by pretending I'm being chased for stealing. Adrenaline running high and coated with soothing sweat, I finally stop within view of the Harlem River, breathing hard, sure that I have left my pursuer in the dust. The river sparkles. Despite the mountains of trash and broken bottles at the foot of a dilapidated, closed bridge, I am elevated and giddy, a feeling usually reserved for my summer visits through the Fresh Air Fund. Sometimes I fantasize that if I make it to the river near the police precinct in record time, the surprise security awaiting me will be my father rather than the cops who hand out lollipops and advice.

Except for a lingering case of the flu, Mom is happy these days, too. Her nausea is my friend, because she's too sick to slink out at night. Maybe she won't find a man as quickly as I found a best friend here. I'm keeping my fingers crossed that she'll keep her legs crossed.

.

7

MIRACLES

In September I started sixth grade with the nicest clothes I've ever owned. A family on my block heard that I have good grades and am a reliable baby-sitter, even though I'm only eleven, so they hired me for a dollar an hour to tutor their two Down's syndrome daughters, Sally and Norah. I much prefer teaching these two strong, rough girls to cleaning and coddling babies. They also pay me exactly what and when they promise.

Because of this job, at the end of September I bought myself a blouse I stalked the entire month. First it was 25 percent off, then 40 percent, and when it plummeted to 60 percent off, I snagged it. Mom raised her eyebrows and clucked when I modeled it at home: "Honey, you look as classy as Audrey Hepburn." On the first day I wore it to school, I also won compliments from my homeroom teacher. When I boasted about buying it with my own money from tutoring, she advised me to hand wash it to make it last longer.

This afternoon I'm pressing the blouse and strenuously creasing my new Wrangler jeans until my mother suddenly unplugs the iron. "Everyone in the living room." I follow her with a sense of dread. Distracted by the possibility that Mom is drunk in the middle of the day, I don't pause to greet Lacey, who has appeared without any advance notice.

After ceremoniously turning off the television, Mom tells us in a hushed, trembling voice that she's not sick with the flu. She's pregnant. Concerned about her poor health, the doctor hinted he could grant her a medical abortion to protect her life. But, no, she couldn't kill a baby.

Joan and Alice hug and kiss her as if this is glorious news; I tighten my fists. "Abortion, abortion!" I urge them all. "We can't have another baby. There's no room. I can tell you now, I'm not helping with another baby." I break down and plead, but they ignore me.

"You're the meanest eleven-year-old alive," Lacey chides me later. "Mom is having a baby and that's that."

That's that. Mom is sick all the time and yells at me that I care more about those retarded girls than my own family. I taunt back: "I care about providing for myself instead of asking welfare or drunken men for money." I will never forgive my mother for balling yet another hit and run father. For the first time in my life, Lacey slaps me in the face; she doesn't approve of me saying Mom is like a fire hydrant male dogs piss all over before completing their business and trotting off. Furious, during class I scribble curses and doodle images of devils and demons in my school notebooks. Keening with shame, I no longer wonder why people hiss the word *welfare* and landlords deny us apartments. We are an infestation.

Once Mom balloons beyond seeing her own feet, she obliges me or Joan to shepherd her on the two buses to the hospital for checkups. I cringe at her tears as she leaves the doctor's office with dire news about her blood pressure and an infection of the placenta. Twice in the middle of the night when she almost chokes on her own vomit, we beg a neighbor to drive us to the emergency room, where people scream in pain for hours and blood and puke pool on the floor. The nurses sneak us hospital food and one doctor tells me it's a pleasure to treat my mom because she speaks English. "But you're as big as a Puerto Rican family," he sympathetically adds. I spit on his pity and the pity I feel for my mother.

One day when I come home late from school, a neighbor has invaded our house to mind Ralph, who's bouncing a ball against the wall, again and again. He won't do anything else and he refuses to go to another room without wailing. Frustrated by Ralph and my late arrival, the neighbor charges. "You wanna know why folks are pouring buckets of water on the street?" Then she blurts out the answer. My youngest sister Alice is in the hospital, maybe dying and definitely brain damaged. En route to a box of Cracker Jacks, she was hit by a car speeding through a stop sign. Her head bounced twice on a manhole cover. The neighbor proudly tells me a specialist has been summoned from another state. I visualize Alice's blood collecting in the decorative cast iron and dripping into the sewer.

Watching Ralph and waiting for news at home, I repeatedly pound the same thought against the walls. It's because Mom is pregnant that six-year-old Alice crossed that street unsupervised. Even if she lives, it's unlikely she'll ever speak again. I fall asleep sitting up on the couch.

My mother shakes me awake; she is laughing, actually laughing, as she identifies this as the most momentous day of her life. Once again we all gather in the living room; this time Mom insists we hold hands. To steady herself as she curls over her own rounded body, unbalanced by deep-throated giggles that seem to come from another person, she carefully reports that the doctor brought in to perform the crane-e-ot-omy had expected to find substantial brain damage from blood buildup. Mom's regular doctor, worried about her making arrangements before enduring a potentially incapacitating labor, advised her to immediately initiate steps to institutionalize Alice.

Instead, during the seven hours of surgery Mom bargained with God. If Alice survived intact, Mom would cease drinking and whoring. She would return to the Catholic Church and resurrect herself as a good mother.

The Lord heard her. Hours after Joan and Lacey fell asleep on hospital benches, the smiling doctor strode across the room and hugged Mom. "When we opened up her head, there was nothing there."

That's when the laughter bubbled up in Mom. When he realized what he had said, the doctor laughed, too, while everyone in the waiting room applauded. Alice, pelvis broken and head squashed on one side, would convalesce in the hospital for months, but her brain did not appear to have sustained any damage. To make it convenient to visit the poor kid, they promised to keep Mom in the hospital as long as possible after she gave birth.

A few evenings later, after hours of leaning on a hospital window to view Alice encased in head bandages and traction,

Mom stands aghast in the street as her water breaks in front of a group of strangers. Rushed back to the clinic, she effortlessly squeezes out another mouth to feed and settles in for the promised week-long rest. She is a queen on a throne of pillows, dazzled that her new jewel, Emma, is as healthy as Alice is ailing. "We impressed those doctors, I can tell you that. We must hail from sturdy peasant stock."

Our strength is sapped by what follows. Quarantined with the measles she catches in the hospital, Alice sinks further into isolation when she cannot recognize Mom's voice on the telephone. Believing that Mom has died giving birth, she becomes a whimpering white mass of casts and sheets.

Alice's tears water Mom's conviction that a miracle has occurred: "The Lord is confronting me with how hurt my kids would be if I left them, and the doctor said I will die if I have any more babies. Eleven pregnancies are too much for this sinner's body. Alice is alive, I'm alive, and we have a healthy new baby. I must prove I deserve this miracle. Everything is going to change."

I believe nothing. Mom makes a lot of promises she can't keep. The only promise that matters to me right now is the one I made to Alice. I vowed to read to her at least three times a week in the hospital, once the quarantine was lifted.

I slink through the black neighborhood to the hospital and then I pay to take the two buses back. Alice looks especially frail in the hospital because I'm not accustomed to seeing any of us in bed alone. I aim to shrink myself to invisibility as I wait for the buses to take me home at night. What if someone jumps me? How many more miraculous survivals will be dispensed to my family?

8

SHAKESPEARE

Initially I thought Emma would die before birth, sucking the life out of Mom and poisoning the rest of us. That she emerged healthy while Alice withered in a hospital bed struck me as a catastrophic coincidence. Lacey whispered to me that Emma's origins were indeed cursed. Emma's father wasn't Wally; he was one of Jackie's hunks who wanted to humiliate her by proving Mom was a drunken whore. Even Lacey's wild, drug-dealing Greenwich Village friends were appalled that her mother got pregnant sleeping with one of her daughters' boyfriends. Surely, nothing good could come out of this.

Superstition is the dust of bad ideas that settles in the crevices of a lazy brain. Mere reason cannot blow it away. I had been absurdly haunted with the notion that Emma was cursed or a source of doom for the rest of us, until the seven-pound-three-ounce bundle confounded expectations. Now I'm coming around to considering her a miracle baby. Her birth salvaged Mom's life without taking Alice's.

For months after Mom and Emma left the hospital, I returned home from school or tutoring convinced that I would find Mom splayed on the couch, drooling like an infant, holding a beer bottle instead of a baby bottle. Like a vulture, I hovered, alert for signs that she had fallen off the wagon. But, true to the promise she made to her Lord in the emergency room, Mom ceased bar hopping and man hunting. Snapping and flaring with less frequency now, her temper subsides before it propels her toward one of us, swearing and ready to slap. Sometimes she boasts that she has a magnificent will; sometimes she tearfully laments her mistakes, expectantly pausing after murmuring, "I deserve to be hated by my children."

I should contradict her, but my throat closes. I'm afraid that forgiveness will melt me into a common mold. I'll become like her, maudlin and prone to sitting for hours in the dark, illuminated only by cigarette embers. I want to live my life the opposite of the way she has lived hers.

When the alarm goes off in the morning, I pop out of bed immediately. I sleep as if I work for the fire department, on call through the night. In these cramped quarters, it's still necessary to share a cot with Joan, but it's important that we not touch. I lie on my back, arms straight at my sides, and push her awake if she starts tossing and turning my way. The warm, electric jolt of another body could strip away the thin veneer of my composure and the fragile surface of my resolve. Touch tricks me into envisioning someone creeping up on me, bald Alice exiled to her hospital bed, and Jackie's boyfriend humping my mother.

Each school morning I tiptoe from the big bedroom, through the living room, into the kitchen. Then I pull the dried clothes off the lines and iron whatever the younger kids need for school. Turning on the kitchen light to the sight of cockroaches scattering is more of a shock each morning than the alarm clock. Snapping a few crunchy shells reminds me of the futility of my efforts at home: we will always be overwhelmed and outnumbered.

Then comes a peace that matters more to me than sleep. With the apartment quiet, I can enjoy being awake. Ironing Joan's dress into crispness gives me great pleasure. With no one talking at me, there's nothing to argue about. I am serene.

This morning I prop open Shakespeare in preparation for English class. We all know why our teacher, who once taught in a college, is now heading a sixth-grade honors class. The thermos he sips from during the day has more than orange juice in it. Once he wets his whistle a couple of times, he ceases to embarrass people by calling on them to explain a line in *Hamlet*. He decries the use of abridged excerpts in our textbooks and displays leather hardcover copies of Shakespeare's works on his desk, dipping into them with as much thirst as he brings to his thermos. Always gesturing toward the prettiest girl in class, he urges us to resist the high-school teachers who will test us on definitions of words and the plots of plays: "Ignore the footnotes and follow your feelings." Culture, he booms through the room, civilizes the expression of emotion. With a beautiful English accent, he recites his favorite monologues and can produce genuine tears on command.

When I find myself crying sometimes for no apparent reason, I chalk it up to something he has recited, like Desdemona pleading with her violently jealous husband, Othello. Books are a fine alibi for inexplicable reactions, like when my eyes blur with tears looking at Emma or Ralph. I can't anticipate the kids' effect on me any more than I can tell when a poem will make me weep or force my heart to palpitate as much as if I'm running uphill.

Last Saturday when Mom went out food shopping without folding up the couch, I stood in the middle of it reading Shakespeare out loud, completely naked, to make it clear that I required an audience of my awed younger siblings to commemorate the future that Joan and I had devised: I would become a spectacularly famous actress. When I am rich and her husband abandons her and her three kids, they will live with me, their favorite aunt.

This particular morning I fail to make it past the living room without rousing Mom. A couple of ashtrays filled with butts at the side of her bed explain her raspy voice. "Honey," she mumbles, "you can go back to bed. It's pouring out. School is closed today. Remember? It's a holiday." I had forgotten. I don't let many details interfere with my routine.

Rain didn't always stop me. Years earlier, I even went out in a hurricane. Mom had woken up to tell me school was closed then, too, but I didn't believe her. By the time I snuck outside, I couldn't admit I was wrong. So I held tightly onto the railings of the stone steps leading up the hill from our street to school. That day there was no reason to be afraid of boys who hid out in the alleys off to the side of the stairs. No one else was out but me and the wind that whipped my hat right off my head. Someone yelled at me from a window, but her words were muffled by the wind.

By the time I arrived at the locked gates of the schoolyard, I couldn't hear anything other than my own sobs.

Then a man draped in a huge yellow raincoat appeared. He whisked me home, muttering in Spanish while he followed my directions and sheltered me from the rain and wind. When he delivered me to my mom, she was sobbing. I didn't tell her or anyone else the reason I had left: if she was pulling my leg and I missed school, I would not ace the Perfect Attendance Award that year. Spelling and attendance were the two things I excelled in. Gold stars and exclamation points from teachers mattered more to me than toys, and almost as much as food.

Why should I have believed her? Sick with the flu one day, I had worried myself sicker because I had books due at the library. Instead of returning them as she promised, Mom threw them out. "That will teach you to care so much about books," she taunted me, as the overdue notices accumulated. "See if that librarian you think is so neat helps you find books now." The librarian erased my debt when I explained how my mom had mistakenly taken the books to the Laundromat, where they were stolen.

Mom was always open to reasons why we should stay home from school: nasty weather, her need for a baby-sitter while she picked up some cash, or our own desire. All you had to do was announce the slightest bellyache, and you could snuggle back under the covers. If Mom felt good, beds became trampolines. You never knew when you would be the one she'd lavish attention on, taking you out to the coffee shop where she sometimes waitressed, treating you to a hamburger or a malt while she smoked and drank coffee with the ladies who lounged in the ripped red-vinyl booths.

Now that I know there really is no school today, I'm squeamish. Pretty soon television and the competing cries and shouts of Emma, Ralph and Alice will turn the volume of the house up too high for me to think. I'll be roped into inept caretaking. Unless I grab the special spanking paddle, I'm unable to control Ralph. He restlessly jumps off furniture or unscrews the knobs on dresser drawers. Alice's frail body and dented head pull on me. I want to do something for her, but I can't identify what. School is my haven.

Fortunately, Paula comes to the rescue, knocking at the door and inviting me to breakfast and then for a ride in her uncle's car. The only noise at her house is the click click of her mother's typewriter earning the money to support Paula and her sister. Until I met them, I thought Jewish fathers never split.

Paula loves reading Shakespeare out loud, too. It's okay when she snickers at my excitement about living on Shakespeare Avenue off a courtyard that is raised slightly above ground level, just like a stage. She joins me in appreciating the spectacle of the street. People exchange recipes, advice and gossip. On Saturday nights when the queens parade downstairs, a few women disapprove, but most are amused that men are the only ones in the building who ever wear evening gowns. Then there are the two handicapped young men who wear diapers. People scratch their heads; what are the odds two young men in the same building will come back from a place called Vietnam in wheelchairs? At twenty-two, Jack returned paralyzed from the waist down and slightly brain damaged. Folks switch his transistor radio for him when he rocks with frustration and they never complain about lifting the wheelchair up and down the stairs. I hear comments about the blessings of veterans' benefits and sorrow for his mother, who has two young children, two older children and now, for the rest of her life, a permanent child to nurse.

If I lived on the third floor in the back, I'd miss important gatherings, like when we all lit candles and sat on the steps mourning JFK. Mom brought us to tears reciting from memory fine things he had said. During the blackout, half the building gathered in the courtyard, sharing candles, flashlights and stories about the punishment awaiting hoodlums who dared to take advantage by grabbing purses and crotches.

Even the small events are interesting. We never know when the obese Polish lady will bring out platters of warm cookies and ramble on about her homeland. No one cares if the two girls she minds are her daughters, granddaughters or nieces. Mysterious relationships are accepted, even when they are violent. There's a lady from Cuba who's perpetually screaming at her oldest kid. At one time or another, everybody has seen this girl run half naked from the apartment, clutching a towel or a nightie, her mother wildly flinging a belt with a big buckle that people speculate would qualify as a weapon if the courts were to interfere. There's something wrong with the father, too, everyone says; he just sits there. We all think this girl is singled out for abuse because she's the only dark-skinned one in the family.

There's an Italian family with six kids, every single one of them beautiful and clean. Their father seems normal, but he's always weary from working two jobs. We can hardly hear his voice when he waves and says hello. Their mother rarely leaves the house except to shop, fetch one of her kids, or attend church. "No time to gossip," she says, even on a warm night when people linger outside past dark. She concocts soup broth from scraps and sews clothing for her entire brood. I thought she was the perfect mother until one day she broke down in the courtyard in front of everyone, informing people she had never spoken to that she was pregnant again and would kill herself this time. She had prayed the growing lump in her belly was a tumor. Catholics and non-Catholics agreed that witnessing her despair could change the pope's mind about birth control.

A Puerto Rican woman, who my mother praises for being devout because she has a shrine in her living room, proudly talks about how she and her husband decided to use rubbers, knowing the Lord would understand they did it out of love for the three children they already had. One day when I bawled in the courtyard, drowning in regret for yelling at Emma that I wished she had never been born, this woman treated me to a movie. She and her family whispered funny translations to make me giggle while they passed the exotic snacks people eat in Spanish-only movie theaters.

In our old neighborhood, nobody ever took anybody else's kids on outings. Here there's a group of single Irish women who transport neighborhood kids all the way to the amusement park in New Jersey, where they pretend to be our mothers. "They are saints," people say, "they double up in bedrooms in order to send small fortunes home to their families."

I wish scads of people weren't moving out to escape the crime. Even Paula's mother has arranged a ride today to hear a presentation and view the site in the Northeast Bronx where over fifteen thousand apartments are being built for people who can't afford to escape to Long Island but can afford two thousand dollars to buy an apartment. Co-Op City may be close to the ocean and a good buy, as she says, but when I see the huge model and posters, I wonder, how is it different from the projects? Ringed by highways and flatness, blocks of elevator buildings will tower over tiny parks. After asking more questions than anyone else in the audience, Paula's mother proclaims the place as shabby as a village built of dominoes. "The buildings will be cheaply built and tumble down one after the other. Folks will regret buying into this swamp."

I'm more worried about those left behind and what it would feel like not to have Paula living down the block from me.

9

FRESH AIR FUND

As I lie next to my first boyfriend at the community pool in
Elmira, New York, I remark that a math genius could not
calculate all his freckles. Commenting on the brown and pink
markings blending into the soft fuzz on his arms provides an
excuse for my eyes to travel the length of his body. His legs and
chest muscle their way into my heart. After years of stiffening my
back and clenching my fists when anyone but Lacey hugs me, I
yearn to touch this boy. But all we ever do is mumble at each
other.

I don't think it is because of the dig about the freckles that
Billy breaks up with me. He seems upset that his mother told him
to stay away from that Fresh Air kid from New York City. She is
one of the mothers who was alarmed that, on days when we
weren't at the pool or the minor league games, I demonstrated
sexy versions of the watusi and frug you'd never see on *American
Bandstand*.

When I was five years old and first started visiting this family in upstate New York during the summer, the whole neighborhood welcomed me despite hearing about my dramatic arrival. As soon as I stepped off the train, I was led behind the station. Hunched over with shame, I submitted to de-licing. A giant woman burned my scalp with a nasty chemical and then scraped off the incinerated lice with a metal-pronged comb. The next day my temporary family assured me that all their neighbors agreed to slap their kids if they called me the Cootie Kid from New York City.

Now that I can shake and bop because Lacey teaches me the latest dances, I'm starting to feel like an unwelcome outsider instead of a protected guest. Going away through the Fresh Air Fund still beats staying home, but this summer for the first time I frequently drift into boredom and flare into anger at some of the people here. They say little, and I don't know how to grab the attention of kids my age except by corrupting them with obscene dances and Spanish curses. Some of them believe that Jewish people have horns. I wonder which one of them Billy will go steady with now that he can only say hello to me.

Easy come, easy go, I remind myself, but I still wonder about his freckles. After I spent hours picking blueberries in the sun and my own freckles came out in full force, accented by all the scratch marks from the bushes, I stared at my own arms and legs wishing they were his.

The mother in the house of my host family is convinced I would find a new boyfriend quicker if my ears didn't devilishly peak through my limp strands. Pretty hair and boyfriends seem to be connected, so I gave in to her entreaties that I experiment with curls. Because I can't venture off the porch with plastic rollers pinching my scalp, I'm flipping through back issues of *National Geographic*, occasionally pressing against pages with a pen and tracing paper. I duck whenever another kid skates or cycles along the road.

Usually I can't sit still on a sunny summer day. I stuff every vase in the house with colorful weeds and flowers I scavenge from a field on the other side of the backyard, or I bike from one clean, sparsely trafficked street to another, defying the rules against going to my favorite destination. Mr. and Mrs. Cranford consider the deserted Remington Rand factory a dangerous eyesore. Windows shattered by idle rocks have been replaced with boards, and glass sprinkles the weeds surrounding the two-story brick structure. Instead of moving on, jobless and disheartened workers linger in the surrounding houses, turning to petty crime and driving recklessly around kids on bikes. My substitute mother doesn't grasp who she is talking to when she warns: "You don't know what goes on there." I'm compelled to pump and sweat my way to the haunting familiarity of the run-down and abandoned.

One rainy night we drove by the factory on the way to the movies, Mr. and Mrs. Cranford in the front seat and me and two of the boys crammed in the back. The front seat noted that the corporation had bowed to community pressure to maintain the lights around the thousands of square feet the building occupied. From the back seat, I admired a glowing replica of a manual typewriter and the black wrought-iron streetlamps that projected halos into the puddles and spotlighted the drain cleaners in luminous yellow raincoats. "It's beautiful," I whispered, and the whole car chuckled at me. I should keep my silly affinities to myself, at home and driving through the world.

Today there will be no gathering or traveling, only this cramped waiting for my hair to dry. Forced to sit still, I dwell on the likelihood that this will be the last summer I come here. Next summer I'll stay in New York and earn some money.

If she was my mom, I would yell at Mrs. Cranford for wasting my time and causing me pain while pulling my hair out of the rollers. Patches of hair that escaped the rollers hang straight next to little ringlets. Shirley Temple I will never be, but I have no intention of being a laughingstock either.

I bolt from Mrs. Cranford lying to me about how cute I look and recklessly race behind the house, where I hose down my head. When she catches me undoing her efforts, she loses her temper with me for the first time in all the years I've visited. Rather than coming across as an ingrate, usually I just say what I know I'm supposed to say to her and she says kind, assuring things to me.

I put up a façade with this family years ago, during my first week as their guest. The lady of the house said, "But where is your favorite doll? Every little girl has a favorite doll," and embarrassed me by dragging her whole family to a toy store when they thought we were about to barbecue.

They laughed when I had protested that I hated dolls and babies, so I knew better than to admit I had no experience picking out a brand-new toy. After we scanned all the shelves stuffed with toys twice, even Mrs. Cranford showed impatience. Jumping with jitters, I pointed to a doll in a white dress, which she bought without checking the price.

75

Although I was trying to fit in, I couldn't play with the doll in the way they encouraged. For weeks, I toted it around in the package every day. When the cellophane window on the box finally broke, I burst into tears: "The doll is going to die." And then, afraid they would ship me home like a damaged package, I couldn't stop sobbing.

Over the years, I have learned that the Cranfords don't welcome the truth, so I've settled into uplifting stories about the Childers children, babbling about how lucky I am to belong to a second family in the summer. But sometimes I make mistakes. They weren't impressed by my ability to decipher forbidden words they spelled from the newspaper as if speaking in an adult code. I shouted "RAPE" after Mrs. Cranford tapped fingers on an open page, one for each letter of the simple word. Then I pounced at the challenge when her husband assured her an eleven-year-old couldn't understand what it meant. "It's when a man throws a woman to the ground and makes her spread and . . ." They shushed me and rolled their eyes at one another.

I agree with them; I shouldn't know such things. But why are we forced to deny what we know? I'd rather be truthful than polite, even if it makes people uncomfortable. Yet I dread the consequences. I'm scalded when people dislike or reprimand me for bad manners, so I aim to be consistently phony. As a result, the three boys and husband completely accept me now, even though I wasn't their idea. I'm a bargain. Mr. Cranford is relieved that his wife no longer talks about longing for a daughter.

This summer she may have realized I'm not blossoming into the girl of her dreams. I'm still an urban tomboy, even though I became fascinated with my freckled boyfriend. Just like my mother, she objects to my reading too much and expects me to give her something not in my possession: lightheartedness. I've disappointed Mom; my oldest and best sister, Lacey; and now this lady, who I'm sure my mother would say is a saint for putting up with me when I'm not even her own flesh and blood.

Late that night, when her husband returns from his repair job with the telephone company, I listen to them quietly picking on each other in their bedroom. People here don't argue the same way they do in the Bronx. You have to listen hard because they don't raise their voices enough to drown out the crickets.

Tonight, after they quibble as usual about his schedule, I'm one of the safe topics of conversation. He makes her laugh about the way I doused my own head of curls and reconciles her to my remaining in New York next summer. I'll be twelve in November and a help to my own family, he murmurs, consoling her that she'll be surrounded by little girls when she resumes teaching the next year.

Suddenly, my heart splinters, and I flinch. Maybe nursery rhymes sing-song us to our personalities. I am Mary, Mary, Quite Contrary. I want them to beg me to come back, despite the fact that I feel little for them after all these years of kindness. Mostly I'm going to miss sleeping and reading in my own room, behind a door that creaks warnings about visitors. In this bed, I feel safe.

My own bed. My own radio. My own clock. Clean curtains. Summer nights sleeping outside in the tent and afternoons playing badminton for hours. Pancakes on Sunday mornings and dessert every single night. Fruits and vegetables adults praise me for gobbling: broccoli and brussels sprouts and green beans. Shelling peas and shucking corn for big parties. Picking flowers.

Mr. Cranford gripes that his wife is a bad cook because "it's the same food week after week," but I think the food here is delicious. At the first picnic they took me to, I stopped eating only when I began to vomit. Nobody had noticed me shoveling olives and deviled eggs and slices of ham and scoops of ice cream down my throat as if I was in a contest. I never ate deviled eggs again, but every year when I returned to New York I missed the food here almost as much as the privacy. Once I'd tasted roast beef, I couldn't swallow the free meat mush we spoon out of a can at home.

As I prepare to depart from their lives, I politely promise to write and to call, if we ever get a phone. They vow to visit me in New York, which makes me panic at the thought that they will discover I have concocted a happy family that just happens to have no money and no father. During the daylong train ride back home, I envision the Cranfords sitting in judgment while Mom smokes and curses. Wouldn't they be surprised that I never mentioned a new baby.

I'm still determined never to forgive my mother for having another baby, but in the reflections of the train window I spot the sun blond hair of my five-month-old sister Emma. With trepidation, I wonder if Alice has managed to regain any weight and if Ralph's broken leg has healed properly. My questions chug along with the train: Is mom still sober? Did she get tied? This train journey rattles me back to a burdensome belonging that I had put aside all summer.

I can't be sure my sisters and brother are looking forward to seeing me. Egged on by Mom, they have christened me "the family flat leaver" because I abandon them every summer.

Years ago my mother had rebuffed the idea of sending any of her kids away through the Fresh Air Fund, but the social worker released a ticker tape of convincing words. Why stick the kids in the Bronx all summer long with nothing to do when there are numerous stable families in upstate New York who want to introduce country life to poor children from the city? The Fresh Air Fund pays for travel; the family provides room and board. Two weeks away from home is a perfect length for a kid, she persisted, without mentioning that some families and kids hit it off so well that the visits stretch to the entire summer.

Mom had urged me to refuse the same way Lacey and Jackie had when they were kids, but as early as the age of five, I was eager for escape, especially because Dad encouraged me to get out of the city while I could. On the day of my departure, afraid we wouldn't wake up on time to catch the ferry and then the train that would transport me to the country, I slept little. At an hour in the morning Mom called ungodly, she clasped my hand all the way to the ferry station, periodically intoning that it was okay to change my mind.

When my name echoed through a loudspeaker, I bounded unhesitatingly toward a new life, until I felt Mom tugging at me across the room. I zigzagged back to hug her and lie: "I'm going to miss you." Then I started to cry. Surrounded by kids, moms and uniformed ladies with badges at the station, almost buckling with premonitions that I would be kidnapped and never see my family again, I instructed my mom that before I returned she should describe that week's hair color. If I immediately spotted her in a crowd, I could purposefully stride past potential abductors.

I didn't cry during the long ride on the Erie Lackawanna train to Elmira that first year and I'm not weeping now, as I return once again to New York, probably for the last time. I stare out the window, grazing the bursting carton of food distributed by the Fresh Air Fund lady. Carrots and cows, melons and meadows, and boys who smell chlorine clean.

10

HUDDLED COUPLES

On a school trip to the Statue of Liberty, my teacher recited the history of Ellis Island and a poem about the huddled masses. But most of the poor people I see huddle in couples or gangs. That the poem was written by a woman named Lazarus made me wish she could rise from the dead for a conversation I knew I couldn't have with anyone else without being dismissed as "negative" and "cynical." I would tell her that the poor people I know fight with one another as much as we undertake difficult, triumphant journeys.

Trudging home from school, gym bag and book bag slung on either shoulder, like the lady emblem of the scales of justice, I spy Alice and Joan. They are huddled outside the apartment, locked out, I guess.

As I zoom closer, I notice that Alice is crying. What's going on now? My mother's voice screams inside me, "I can't take it anymore," and then her snicker when I exaggerate vibrates inside me, too.

"Better not go inside," Joan warns.

I couldn't have, even if I wanted to. Jackie's boyfriend Bad News is hogging all the space in the doorway. At first it looked like he was barging out. Then he pivoted, grabbing the top of the doorframe, as if bracing himself for fifty pull-ups. "He's one strong bastard," I've heard Mom say. He has spent more time in gyms than classrooms.

The whole neighborhood can probably hear his booming voice. "I'll kill you the next time, Jackie, I swear. You'd better learn the difference between being nice to my friends and flirting. Never again, or you'll be sorry."

Then he's backing away, with Mom coming at him wearing a bloodied housedress and swinging a cast-iron frying pan. She wields her all-purpose weapon as if it weighs nothing: "Who the fuck do you think you are threatening, you punk? Don't forget, I know your father would never lay a hand on a woman. You get out of here and never come back. I'll turn you in. You want scars on the other side of your face, too? Don't make me call the cops on you, buddy."

He plants his feet straight together and flings his arms down to his sides, like a gymnast sticking a landing, as if that will startle any opponent. He doesn't know who he is dealing with. Mom sober is a force to be reckoned with. Once when a woman screamed late at night in the courtyard, "Don't cut me, don't cut me," Mom fearlessly ran out of the house yelling that the police were on their way. The next day she lectured the air within hearing distance of neighbors: "We promised we would never forget Kitty Genovese." They had frequently discussed the nurse in Queens who was stabbed to death while her neighbors ignored her cries for help. After a while, when they referred to Kitty it felt like we were mourning someone we knew.

Today Mom jumps in front of Jackie's boyfriend. "Stay away from my daughter. Anything happens to her, I'll haunt you the rest of your life, *and* I'll haunt you in the afterlife. I've been nice to you, but I can be a monster when I need to be."

Except for her belly, Mom is skinny—frail, even. But she's a Herculean monster, capable of getting the best of him, even without a frying pan. He's backing down and strutting toward his car as if he doesn't notice people sighing in the courtyard, "Hope nobody is hurt," and hooting, "You tell him, Sandy."

Inside, Jackie resembles a pile of laundry crumpled in a corner. "I thought he loved me," she cries, lifting her head. Her nose and upper lip swollen and one eye shut, blood caked in her blond hair and around one ear, she is unrecognizable.

Joan sputters: "I never told you because I thought you'd yell at me, but me and Alice saw him holding hands with another girl!"

Mom gently discourages Joan from hovering around Jackie. "That's history. Jackie doesn't need to hear you tell tales now."

Transforming herself into dead weight to make it harder for Mom to drag her away, Joan props herself against the wall. She tries again to make Jackie angry at Bad News so that she'll rise from the corner like a champion who cannot be felled for long: "He's a no-good ladies' man."

Mom cackles: "It's a good thing we're not ladies." I guess she realizes that Joan won't budge before Jackie, so Mom indulges her instead of pulling: "The things that come out of your mouths crack me up sometimes." While advising Jackie to make her way over to the couch, Mom trills: "I need a Florence Nightingale to fill up a pot with warm water and find some clean towels that have seen better days."

Rather than utter the frightening word *hospital,* I follow Mom's cue, taking a chance that she's too focused on Jackie to misinterpret me. "Okay, Monster!"

Mom crows. "I must have made quite a spectacle of myself, heh? I'm only a monster when I'm a mom who has to fight for her kids." She's looking pleased with herself even while she's settling Jackie on the couch. "Does that make me a Monster who scared away the Mobster?"

Chortling, Ralph prompts Alice to jump up and down, clasping hands and swinging their arms. They sing, "Mom is a momster who scared away the mobster."

"He was so embarrassed, he reddened like a lobster," I add, chanting rather than singing.

Jackie's whole body convulses while she stretches out. "Don't make me laugh, it hurts everywhere," she happily pleads with us. Her fighting spirit revives. "Do you believe that bastard punched me? What a coward!"

All of us yell "Bastard!" and punch the air, confident that Mom won't object. She's proud when we cohere in times of trouble, cheering one another on.

Sometimes it is true that delight follows disaster just like day follows night. But I'm afraid that for a long time the bathroom cabinet will mirror back to Jackie the disaster of this day.

We all thought Jackie and her boyfriend would marry—and then make each other miserable, of course. He was Bad News and she was impossible to live with, but miracles do happen, Mom would say hopefully to no one in particular.

On Mom's forty-second birthday, Bad News paid for all of us, including Lacey and Dana, to celebrate at a fancy restaurant on Arthur Avenue, the Italian neighborhood near Alexander's Department Store and a big Catholic university. He insisted on seating the boy of the family next to him. Every once in a while he asked Ralph a question, chucked him under the chin or promised he would teach him how to throw a ball. But then he and Jackie hardly paid attention when we sang "Happy Birthday" to Mom and sniffed her perfumed corsage in tribute.

They disappeared into one another like a honeymoon couple. Arms braided together and chair legs interlocking, they acted like a two-headed turtle all night, hiding in their shell to keep everyone else away.

I whispered to Lacey that they were being rude to Mom and she sniped: "They're in love and they're stoned. Expect nothing. Be grateful that they aren't angry at each other and stoned, or in love and in withdrawal. That would be an ugly sight."

Lacey's words conjured the ugliest spectacle I'd ever seen: what she looked like after her stomach was pumped following an overdose a year ago. The hollows of her eyes darkened like aged coffee stains and her cheekbones jutted out as prominently as a skeleton's. For weeks she shook and cursed while suffering from withdrawal from speed and heroin. When people squawk about the smack and crime epidemic in Spanish Harlem, across the river from us, I recall a newspaper photo of addicts slumped against garbage cans. That image distracts me from smelling the vomit and fear of Lacey's jones.

I hope overdosing and becoming a dyke aren't the way Jackie exorcises Bad News. Maybe Mom being sober means she'll help Jackie instead of heckling her the way she did Lacey in the Tommy era.

Cooking in the kitchen, I hear them in the living room singing along to love songs. Then the foyer echoes with the overlapping lines of a round they are shouting instead of singing, engaged in a debate in which everyone agrees about the nature of men.

You can't live with them, you can't live without them.

Too bad men are such bums.

Too bad men are such scumbags.

They'll promise anything but a real conversation.

Love 'em and leave 'em but don't grieve 'em.

The only thing men give you that lasts is children.

When Mom remembers that Ralph probably understands what they are saying but not why, she comforts him. "We don't mean you, honey. You're not like other boys; you're quiet and good and you love your mother."

In truth, Mom fears that Ralph won't last to manhood. He's accident prone, frequently falling and knocking himself black and blue. He often cuts his fat fingers by inserting them into the triangular openings of evaporated milk and tomato sauce cans. Once, I caught him diligently scraping his arm with a can opener and lifting shreds of skin with a nail clipper.

We try to include him, but he can only sit still with us for short periods of time. He edges up next to Alice and Joan, staring at them while they talk, until he is propelled to kick and punch. "Look at him, he's more comfortable sitting close to the TV for

86

hours than to us," Mom teases. "Do you believe he is four already, but stuck in the terrible twos?"

Brooding about Jackie's bruised face and Mom's bruised life, I think that maybe we all go through life searching for the perfect couple but settling for terrible twos.

11

BIRTHDAYS

For years now, a week or two before my mid-November birthday, I team up with Mom to rescue her from a self-induced frenzy. Like someone with no memory, she rattles with irritation that the welfare check and her odd jobs won't cover rent, utilities, food and presents. Some practical joker must have devalued the dollar without notifying the citizens. She's overwhelmed by the fact that the cost of notebooks increases faster than the back-to-school welfare allowance. Each September, somebody or other needs new shoes. In October, Ralph's birthday, then Lacey's and then Jackie's in quick succession empty her spirit and her wallet. Not until the end of October does she calculate the dollars drained from her wallet by Halloween costumes right before the extras needed for Thanksgiving and for gifts at Christmas. "What do you kids expect me to do with the pittance the Man gives me? If I buy any of you one more thing, I'll miss too many Christmas Club payments. Then we'll all be sorry."

Behind her back I imitate Connie Francis singing "Who's Sorry Now?"

My odd chore is to salvage the situation in early November by refusing to celebrate my birthday. After three birthdays in October, who needs to lick frosting out of a bowl in November, too? Unlike the rest of my family, I've had my share of presents—from the Cranfords. Once they understood that my siblings manhandled my gifts before I had a chance to lose interest in them, they had waited until each summer to present me with a bike, hardcover books and brand-new clothing. They weaned me from anticipating a birthday in November. Besides, between tutoring the endearing Down's Syndrome twins and pushing the broom and emptying the trash for the pickled janitor at the Catholic school two nights a week, I'm bringing in enough cash to wear a different skirt to school every day of the week.

I spare Mom the expense of my birthday so that I can lower the buzz of her worry and prevent her from wasting welfare money on something cheap that she thinks I'm old enough to want: clotted mascara, vinyl pumps, padded bras and plastic barrettes my thin hair can't hold. I also spare her because it is better to give in than to receive what costs someone else too much. It makes me feel sad and powerful that I allow her to manipulate me into doing what's right, but I certainly have no qualms about the way I intend to manipulate her today.

Joan and I shuttle back and forth.

"You ask."

"No, you."

"You, c'mon."

It doesn't bode well that Joan returns from talking to Mom so quickly. "There's no cake and frosting mix because she's just too tired to make a cake. Her arthritis is killing her."

Joan typically needs prodding to hustle back from the front lines with adequate intelligence. "Was she angry that you asked? Is she broke?"

Other words churn inside me: how could Mom not even bother telling us that she planned to ignore Emma's first birthday?

But I'm trying to be productive, not provocative. "Should I volunteer?" I compose myself for the approach, reviewing the ammunition that should be released only as a last resort.

I still cringe when I think of the far-from-immaculate conception that preceded Emma's birth. I doubt that Mom will ever again do anything as crass as sleeping with one of Jackie's boyfriends. But she might spontaneously and instinctively punish Emma for her origins; a parent's shame and love sometimes collide and accidentally flatten a child. Still wincing with guilt that I had wished Emma dead, offering her a deferred welcome into the world via a birthday party feels like my duty. I can't control births, but sacrificing my own birthday sanctions my demand that the miracle baby be celebrated.

Having rehearsed the moves I hope not to use, I inch into the living room where Mom does most of her living. "Mom, Joan said you're too tired to make a cake for Emma's first. I'll shop, bake and clean up; Joan will help. We can skip presents, but . . ."

"You're such a dear. Can you bring me my purse?" Lying on the couch, scrounging for bills in her purse, Mom looks old. She used to fuss with her hair; now she ignores the patches of baldness mowed by years of cheap hair dye. Nothing she swallows cures the vitamin deficiency precipitated by multiple pregnancies and scads of bad habits. Her breasts and stomach droop, and thick, curly hairs unfurl from her moles. She looks tired, but also contented, as she hands over the cash for my shopping spree. "It's not much, but it'll cover the mix and some ice milk. Get the vanilla, chocolate, strawberry combo, will ya?"

I revved up for a battle Mom no longer initiates but I still expect, like a rescued, abused puppy that can't trust its new owners. Maybe because she wants me to forget the two years she was a druggie, Lacey advises me to keep up with the calendar. I'm supposed to relate to mom A.D.—After Drink, and ignore the longer period of our lives together B.S.—Before Sobriety. My personal family album is stuck on a track that jumps and screeches away from the possibility of harmony. Like a priest, I will withhold absolution until I am convinced she is sufficiently contrite about her sins and unlikely to lapse back into her old ways.

Lacey drives all the way from Queens for Emma's birthday party. When she learns that I baked the cake and depleted my Halloween booty to buy real ice cream, she's obviously pleased. "What a little woman you are becoming." She gushes about the fact that I'm menstruating and wearing a bra now, as if they are an individual achievement connected to the ability to bake. But I know what actually pleases her. She's relieved that someone else is absorbing some responsibility for the younger kids. Part of why she got hooked on drugs was to escape feeling solely responsible for the family. I reluctantly accept the baton of the big sister. Maybe I'll smash windows with it and leapfrog out of here.

Mom leads us in a prayer of thanks that we're all alive and

happy. She rocks Emma in her arms on and off all day and coos that her shit smells like roses. The cake is perfect, none of her daughters are dogs, and her son is brilliant. Lacey no longer touches those awful drugs, thank God! Mom particularly praises Jackie. "People pay a fortune to pour Jackie's gorgeous hair color out of a bottle" and "Jackie can talk a blue streak and charm the pants off anyone." Mom's laughter cancels the pain of her arthritis for a day and carries the party.

Since she stopped drinking, there's a new calm to the way we live, despite the flare-ups about money and crime. None of our celebrations ends with drunken tears, arguments or furious departures. Only a month ago Lacey, Joan and Mom coordinated the biggest birthday party we've ever thrown in our house. It was a happy occasion, despite the way it began for Alice.

Lured out of the house to shop for a pair of jeans with Joan, Alice returned home wilted and weary. She was empty-handed and hungry, as planned. Enduring something humdrum would convince Alice that no one remembered her birthday, despite her hinting and prodding from the beginning of February. "How many more days before I'm seven?"

Based on the expertly arranged shrine of presents in the living room when Joan ushered Alice in, this birthday was all that Lacey had been thinking about for a month, too.

At just about the same time, we all managed to shout "Surprise! Surprise!" Shy, as if she had wandered into someone else's house, Alice stepped forward slowly, brightening at the colorful packages and then, appearing ready to pass out, noticed the bike. Straddling her first bike, stopping occasionally to stroke its gleaming metallic blue handles and silver sparkles, she unwrapped three presents tentatively, looking around as if to see who they truly belonged to and where they came from. In some households, "Where do presents come from?" is a more perplexing question than "Where do babies come from?"

Walking backward while keeping her eyes on the bike, Alice plopped down next to Mom to open a box of seven pairs of underwear, each with a different day of the week stitched across the butt in an array of pastel colors. I hoped she wouldn't make the same mistake I did at her age. On receiving my labeled week of underwear, I assumed each pair would be clean on the corresponding day, and my life would fall into order. But their promise of predictability apparently did not make as much of an impression on Alice as their violation of her privacy. When the boy who lives in the adjacent apartment approached her with his present, Alice's face reddened and her eyes muddied. She scooped up her underwear and zigzagged past her bike, yelling "Wait, wait, I'll show you!"

Quickly reappearing, she stuffed her embarrassing gift under a pot she had fetched from the kitchen and turned upside down. Then she banged a big aluminum spoon on the upturned bottom of the pan, offering another spoon to the friend who had inspired her modesty. Soon the two of them synchronized thumping the pot and singing "Happy Birthday! Happy New Year!" Her clanging disruption of the party was tolerated because it was her birthday, but most faces expressed dismay.

As I observed Alice, I was sure that this precious, peculiar child was banging out an important message. For months following her return home from the hospital, she had calmly and quietly endured life as if it were a series of medical tests. But now she wanted to dramatically celebrate her existence despite everything that had happened.

Alice's return to kindergarten, bald and shrunken, would have shaken up most kids. Day after day older kids taunted her, "Bald, bald, skinny Minny / Can't say if her dad is old or guinea." Some asked if she was going to a concentration camp again the coming summer. Others challenged her: "Why didn't you just die and get it over with." One offered to kill our cat so that Alice could have a wig. Confused by medications, she said nothing when kids stole stuff from her cubby when she went to the bathroom; she lacked the confidence to declare what she brought each morning. By the time the teacher noticed the commotion around Alice and assigned an aide to accompany her during recess, too many kids had become accustomed to punishing Alice for her appearance.

Alarmed after a hospital checkup, Mom had whispered to me and Joan about Alice's possibly stunted growth and organ damage. She weepily told Alice that her hair and body might not grow anymore, and then didn't know what else to do but accept the tissue Alice offered her. As efficiently as she knew how, Alice comforted Mom and herself. "I'm so lucky. If I'm not going to grow, I don't have to go to school."

No one could change her mind. Although she was practically born chatting, about school she would say only "I don't go to school."

When her teacher initiated regular visits with little assignments, Alice welcomed her as if she were another member of the family rather than a representative of the site of her humiliation. Without prompting, my little sister recruited us to help her read her very own books the teacher netted through a special city program. Just as calmly, Alice announced one day that she planned to attend first grade like other kids. Then she bowed and showed us her skull: it was decorated with shoots of growth as slender and promising as wicks on birthday candles.

12

A NEW APARTMENT

When Mom stopped drinking, she started planning again. Acknowledging that the two-bedroom Shakespeare Avenue apartment was too small for us and that the landlord would never correct the frequent flooding in the apartment above, she undertook a quest for an affordable three-bedroom. Grateful for leads from neighbors, she hounded local landlords who were torn between their reluctance to shelter welfare families and to forgo rent on apartments abandoned by white flight. Soon after Alice's birthday, we moved into a grand three-bedroom apartment on the top of a hill overlooking a park just five blocks from Shakespeare Avenue.

The move was an ordeal Mom still hasn't recovered from a month later. Her black and blue marks show no signs of fading and she curls her shoulders forward to reduce the pain. Dana, Lacey, Jackie and Mom had spent two days dragging furniture up the hill on a dolly and then up the stairs to our new place. The rest of us hauled empty drawers, cushions and boxes of clothes and kitchen supplies.

As each big piece of furniture settled against a wall, Mom reminisced about its origins. "It's French. Hard to believe someone would give away a piece with so much detail. It takes blood, sweat and tears to carve flowers without the wood splitting." I chiseled into her good mood by pointing to unmatched knobs and the drawer that wouldn't close all the way. Despite years of promising not to collect any more heavy furniture, Mom can't pass up a bargain at Goodwill or a chest of drawers abandoned on the street for the first comer.

We rode our seesaw of gratitude and complaint until it was time for balance and levelheadedness to link us. Mom conceded on the effect of the hodgepodge of styles. "We're living in a secondhand store!"

I yielded, in turn. "You're right; wood furniture beats plywood." She made me admit that sometimes the grain and design of a particular piece of furniture make it worth lugging around, but I had to add: "as long as we stay put for a while."

Lacey and Dana seconded my prayer. "Amen!" They had been real sports, helping Mom pack and then carrying the heaviest furniture themselves, proud of their strength. "Who needs a man when you're already a workhorse?"

Mom insists on sleeping in the living room so that her girls can have the two big bedrooms and her boy a small room all to himself. Emma encamps in a crib near the couch, so there's almost always someone to play with her. Because Jackie, in Mom's lingo, rarely deigns to visit, Alice enjoys the privacy I crave, although Mom still checks on her several times a night without knocking. Despite Alice's growing hair and body, Mom fears that some surprise brain activity may hijack Alice's life while she sleeps.

Joan and I love the room we share. The former tenants left painted shutters on our two sets of floor-to-ceiling windows. Finally, we are princesses. From the streets Joan yells up at me to let out my golden brown hair, and I dangle a rope with messages all the way down the four flights. Late at night we still soothe each other with protestations of Best Friends Forever, but we're most transported by songs about everlasting love.

Settling into the apartment turns out to be easier than getting used to the building and our block. On nights when the radiators spew too much heat, the kids walk around in underwear. I itch with discomfort because my modesty keeps me covered, as if, I'm teased, I have something to hide. We crack open the windows and submit to noises that steal the sweetness from our dreams. People blast stereos without regard for neighbors, and no one dares object. Addicts snooze all day and exercise their lungs at night, bellowing greetings, curses and deal breakers. The thunder of bongos and lightning threats of gang members bolt across the street from the park, where Puerto Ricans and blacks have staked out different sections. Irish cops out of uniform sometimes show up to instigate fights over who owns the swings and basketball courts. Dominicans increase tension by elbowing the space of the Puerto Ricans. The more people fight, the less there is to fight over. When it's cold, the night owls and party people burn benches that are never replaced; the city no longer bothers to clean the park bathrooms.

My first association with a knife is that it is a weapon, not a utensil. I close my eyes tightly, like the shutters on my bedroom windows, when I remember the streaks of blood in the hall where an elderly woman unwisely clutched her purse against the demands of a knife-wielding punk. But knives are falling out of fashion. Increasingly, guns are what we should fear.

With the park off limits, Joan spends hours on the sidewalk outside the house. One Saturday I leave for my tutoring session with Sally and Norah after teasing her for playing hopscotch with kids three years younger than herself. When I return several hours later, she is still there, jumping rope and chalking up the sidewalk with eight-year-olds. In front of her new friends, I yell that she should grow up and help Mom with the laundry on a Saturday instead of playing like a baby. Chalk marks on her butt and dirt smudged on her reddened face, she sprays me like a bursting fountain of wisdom: "What's so good about growing up? Boys bother you and you're expected to be clean all the time."

I leave her alone because I'm wiped out from my tutoring, which consists mostly of wrestling the twins for attention despite knowing they forget everything I teach them within two weeks. I have to believe there is hope for Joan, but I'm worried. She jumps at the chance to stay home from school and would watch cartoons all day every day if she could. As if she's still a little girl, she carries her Chatty Cathy doll around to start conversations with other kids on our block, viewing everyone as a potential friend.

The graffiti-scarred halls of our building are almost as dangerous as the park. If bad weather hits, punks from the park seek shelter inside surrounding buildings. When we were moving in, we couldn't leave anything unattended for even a second. We played a relay game to safely deliver everything we owned while creepy guys smoked weed under the stairs, occasionally coming out from under to check us out and slur welcomes. "That's a lot of sisters." "Who teaching that boy to be a man?" "We'd help if we could stand, ladies."

The first day we were moving in, Joan, Alice and Ralph played hide-and-seek in the corridors connecting the two main entrances. But they quickly learned to use only the main entrance near the stairwell leading to our apartment. Even though the lock on the vestibule door is broken, we press the bell as soon as we enter the hall, speak into the intercom as if an adult has responded to our ring, and then hightail it upstairs. I may not believe in God, but I believe in boogeymen.

I sense them everywhere in the long walks I take around the West Bronx, haunted by rumors of gang rapes that don't make the papers. I hope people are exaggerating our jeopardy. The rumble of trucks moving white people away from the neighborhood leaves me feeling as abandoned as when my father split. It turns out I inaccurately predicted what I would most miss about the Cranfords. It's not the bedroom or the food; it's feeling safe meandering or biking through the streets. How could we not have known that we were moving uphill to danger? No one warned Mom that the sliver of green space we admired from our windows was the territory of untended, noxious human weeds. We're sinking in the same swamp as the rest of the regular folks who live here: Puerto Rican, black, Jewish, Irish and Italian families attached to spacious, affordable apartments and the neighborhoods that surround them. Once intimately linked to Manhattan by a stately bridge from the nineteenth century that gave this area the name Highbridge, our isolation and demise are now represented by that defunct, crumbling structure, closed even to foot traffic now in order to deter crime.

An old lady who moved here in the fifties and now is afraid to leave her apartment at night tells us that this neighborhood was once like a suburb, only better. You could rent big apartments with views and skip the worry of maintaining a house. "The West Bronx was part of the Art Deco movement," she says, and I wonder when the decks crumbled and disappeared. She rambles on about a design craze for apartment homes that would ease the domestic burden on women. Now Riverdale is the part of the Bronx the wealthy choose.

Wouldn't you know that neighborhoods deteriorate just as we discover them? We're the John the Baptists of Urban Decay, alerting our fellow man to what's coming. Once the white trash moves in, it's nothing but poor colored families after that. Then landlords stop making repairs and building inspectors go blind, even though these buildings are worth fighting for in a way our old tenement wasn't. Because of vandalism and theft, Catholic churches now barricade their doors except when they are holding Mass. It figures that churches are closed most of the time just when my Mom has returned to the fold.

Lobbies in distant neighborhoods, like Riverdale, have become my churches. Instead of votive candles and illuminated altars, some glow from fireplaces with electric logs. I have staked out a few where people don't balk at my sitting quietly and reading as if I'm in my own living room. When I'm hot from walking, if no one is around I rip open my jacket, lift my shirt and crush my chest against the cool marble walls.

13

THE WATCH

My most treasured possession during my first year of junior high school is the watch I found in a bathroom and never turned in. Now I can chart a day with precision. If chatter ignites into commotion first thing in the morning at home, I slip out the door when it's still dark. Then I kill time and stay warm ducking into hallways during my carefully delayed arrival at school. Just a few incidents of mockery for wearing a skimpy spring coat in cold weather made me want to hide, especially after I made a fool of myself defending my coat's lining as if it had feelings: "It is warm! It is!" A last-minute dash into the schoolyard means I don't have to painfully lock my body against shivering and against the throngs of kids. Adults with ill intent attack at night, adolescent bullies during the day.

Today, one minute I am dazzled by the sparkling icicles dangling from the occasional tree, and the next I'm stabbed by daggers of cold. Tears freeze like tinsel on my eyelashes while a bus loaded with kids slowly grinds up a hill. For a change, I wish I were crushed in with them.

The streets are too slippery for my usual trot, and I am shaking by the time I get to school. A storm of accusations thunders in my brain most of the walk. It's not fair that just four blocks southeast from me anyone who goes to this school receives a free monthly bus pass. Other kids farther away in better neighborhoods are issued passes even if they live in fancy buildings and have working fathers. Lugging my books and tilting on the remainders of boot soles, I indulge in indignation. There *must* be a way to snare the money for next month's pass from my mother or from one of the neighbor ladies who owes me for baby-sitting. It might help to bang my head against a streetlight: it's so stupid of me to spend money on headbands and matching knee socks instead of buses, stupid, stupid, stupid.

Cold and shaken to distraction by the time I face the school door, I don't realize until third period that I dropped the watch instead of hiding it in my book bag as usual. Through the next two periods I hear nothing but my own screaming plan: *as soon as the lunch bell rings, scramble to the yard before the watch is picked up or crushed.* After a morning of courting invisibility, I make a spectacle of myself dashing out of class, coat and book bag trailing.

Kicking the slush in the area where I remember shoving the watch in my bag, I discover instead a plastic holder with this month's bus pass. I know its owner as a wearer of Capezio shoes who boasts about weekend shopping sprees with her rich big brother. The watch didn't have a name on it, the pass does. My conscience solemnly registers: this would be stealing.

All through lunch I chew on my moral dilemma, which is more satisfying than food. Although I don't mind the free lunch at school, I'm embarrassed to be the only kid from the accelerated program in the cafeteria. All the other white kids who eat free lunch are in the two, three and four classes; the only black girls who will sit with me are basketball players, and they are always surrounded by black guys whose intentions are impossible to decipher. Are they flirting or threatening? Is it rude to ask someone to repeat himself when I can't understand what he's said and condescending to nod when I'm lost in the conversation? To avoid lunchroom tribulations, I linger at the nearby soda fountain where kids are allowed to bring a sandwich as long as we buy a beverage.

Sometimes, determined to fatten up, I splurge on a malt. But usually, while my few friends from class order lunch, I select Lipton tea, which costs less than soda or iced tea. The other kids tease me about my strict diet of cheese sandwiches. No way would I tell them about the rectangular blocks of cheddar cheese available free each month to welfare recipients or admit that cans of tuna and packages of cold cuts are what we buy for dinner, not lunch. There is so much that can't be said, I'm happy to stare silently at mahogany walls and gleaming, polished brass fixtures while I decide that I will return the bus pass next week.

The following day I feel like a queen riding the bus to school once I overcome the initial fear at flashing the pass at the bus driver. Then I am suddenly deposed. When my homeroom teacher asks if I used someone else's bus pass that morning, I lamely reply. "Yes sir, I found it on the street and thought I might as well use it." He marches me over to its owner.

I'm not welcome at the lunch counter anymore. One of my former friends sneers that everyone always knew I was a thief. It was obvious that I had something to hide. I'm not surprised by her switching sides; she had wavered about liking me ever since the day I told her, intending to be helpful, that her cleavage looked like an anthill. Trimming her bangs that morning, she hadn't noticed hundreds of tiny, dark brown slivers sifting and clinging to her large breasts. "What are you doing staring down my blouse?" she had snapped.

Within days I find a delicious peace during my friendless lunch hours in exile. I sneak into lobbies of apartment buildings around school to eat my cheese sandwich or walk around when the weather cooperates, craning my neck to ogle these queer, gaping-mouth creatures called gargoyles perched on rooftops. I memorize William Wordsworth's "Tintern Abbey," the beautiful words seducing me into being a lover of the buildings and the streets and the hills. Without a watch to alert me when to turn back, I dwell within a seven-block area. In the Bronx, as in Elmira and in empty churches, I can be lulled by Wordsworth's "sublime mood." There are flowers in poems and peace in "the quiet of the sky." Words fall from the sky or the page, clinging close to my bosom.

At the same time, my schoolwork is suffering. I no longer enjoy shouting out answers to verbal math problems when other kids are still scribbling. Rather than paying attention, in most of my classes I secretly read poetry or schlock novels about nurses and stewardesses.

I can't predict my grades after a test and studying doesn't seem to make a difference. My concentration often weakens and I turn

105

pages like an automaton. I read like someone who hasn't noticed she's riding in a car in a deep fog. No matter what the density of the air or information, I continue at the same speed until I realize I don't quite know where I am. The context has disappeared. The light of my mind blinks and cranks up a notch in search of some startling illumination, but often the light glares too close. Again and again, some points seem bigger than they are and I no longer have perspective. I reach the end of my journey with little memory of where I have been, knowing only that sad poems are the best companions.

Forging Mom's signature on my report cards deepens my discomfort in school, especially now that I'm known as a thief, but I can't break the habit that started years ago. I once stood in a narrow darkened hallway lined with dressers that were piled with clothes and a jumble of other things: a checkerboard, newspapers and a hairnet. Mom leaned over the sink, elbow deep in suds, ducking the clothing lines overhead. She screamed that she didn't have the time to sign my report card. I protested that I would get in trouble if I did not hand it in with her signature. Sighing and rolling her eyes, she dried her hands and let me approach.

I don't know why I was forcing her to sign then rather than at a more convenient time for her. I don't know if there was a more convenient time or how many times I had already urgently asked. For some reason, I was desperate to have her notice my A's. She signed without saying a word. Ever since then, to avoid a showdown, I usually forge her signature on perfectly good report cards, nervous about getting caught while knowing I have nothing to hide.

I still attend school more than Joan and Alice, but once there I often fade into anxious absence. Sometimes I swipe a banana at the corner grocery store and then ignore the teacher in order to listen for a telltale pounding on the door. I assume the police have been informed I am a thief and now they are watching me. They should. I await the time when I'll do something so terrible I'll be kicked out of school and end up like Lacey and Jackie after all.

Even though she has a job with benefits, Lacey tells me dropping out of school was a huge mistake. "If you have a college degree, you can be an idiot and they'll put you in charge," she complains. I console myself with *Daily News* stories of men who earn college degrees while serving time.

14

GRAND CONCOURSE

Last summer I was still a child, now I am an honest-to-goodness teenager. I'm twelve and have my first full-time job. Fifteen dollars a week isn't a fortune, but I'm confident I can save for a winter coat although I haven't yet settled on where to stash the cash. Mom and Jackie wouldn't be able to resist raiding my old piggy bank and rifling though my pockets if they smelled a surplus in the apartment.

Five days and two nights a week I baby-sit an eighteen-month-old boy while his mother shops, disappears in curlers under the cave of a hair dryer for an hour at the beauty parlor, or supervises the decorating of her enormous apartment on the Grand Concourse. Whenever the weather is good enough to escort Ira outside, I pretend I'm strolling down the boulevards of Paris I've seen in travel brochures. Then we loll in the park two blocks from his apartment. I know this is the closest I will ever come to living on the Park Avenue of the Bronx.

As the weeks pass, I settle into my new summer routine. I'm glad I didn't go to Elmira through the Fresh Air Fund this summer; being watched like a child makes me more uneasy than having to mind one. In this job I relish the freedom of being on my own most of the day, but I'm uncomfortable with Ira and his mother. Neither tickling, nor giggling, nor stretching my rubber face, nor dangling a colorful toy draws much of a reaction from him. Not that I should complain. Because he sleeps or stares mutely at the sky as I rock his carriage, I'll be able to read all the Nancy Drew books I borrowed.

Even his mother doesn't seem attached to this lump of a child. Every morning when I arrive, always punctually, she seems eager to escape. Sometimes she stops by the park to cuddle him, but mostly she stops by to check up on me. She's afraid I'm neglecting her son and having too much fun with the neighborhood boys who have started to flock around me. If it's not raining, they can count on me for chatting, bike watching, and relaying messages. I've become a gathering place and a teenage kiosk. "Don't let me catch you with more than three other kids at any time, you hear me?" Mrs. Wood warns.

This lady knows her hands, nails and clothes are perfect, but deplores the rest of her life. Her husband begrudges her a mother's helper, she gripes, and won't move to Westchester County, where her friends own houses. He's not bothered by the neighborhood changing and by some of her friends refusing to visit. When I hear her complaining on the phone about her husband working exorbitant hours, I smirk with conviction that he deliberately delays returning home.

Driving me home late one Saturday night, Ira's father praises my reliability and volunteers marital advice: "Word to the wise. Don't always push your husband to make more money. Happiness should come from inside and from your children." Usually silent, he must be inspired by a night of alcohol and arguing.

"You don't have to worry about me driving any man crazy, I intend to be an old maid," I counter matter-of-factly. Only a single silhouette in a desiccated landscape fills this girl's crystal ball. My horizon is a desert populated by warning signs: Don't have babies; Avoid depending on anyone; Watch out for traps.

For the first time, I hear this man laugh. It occurs to me that he was once a teenager. I learn that he is thirty-one and shocked that he married someone who would insist on a sunken living room. Taking a risk, I comment, "I understand wanting a sunken living room. It's the nicest room I've ever spent more than a half hour in. I just can't understand not letting Ira roll around the rug there."

Most days Ira and I wander outside, sometimes for six hours straight. The friends who have drifted into my life are willing sentinels; they conduct surveillance and whittle down the crowd to three when they spot Mrs. Wood or someone they mistake for her coming our way. To antagonize her, Jason, the one black guy in the crowd, sticks by my side. He's not allowed to touch Ira, but even she doesn't have the nerve to forbid me his company. Her bigoted comments about the colored make me want to blurt out that Jason attends the Bronx High School of Science and is smarter than Ira will ever be, I can tell you that. But I keep my mouth shut.

The one and only time this lady drove me home after I babysat on a Saturday night, she insisted on meeting my mother.

After complaining about walking up four flights of stairs, she paraded her disgust down our hallway. "What's that smell?" she wheezed. "How can you stand to live here?"

An answer crawled in my throat: If I unleash roach spray in your face, you'll never have trouble identifying that smell again.

Now that Mom prays regularly, she reminds me that we have benefited from charity and should reciprocate, especially with annoying people. When I practice empathy, I can see that this lady is lonely, disappointed and oblivious to her good fortune. Being better off doesn't mean better, and I'm becoming confused about who is rich. The Cranfords live in a house, but even with overtime they could afford vacation only every other year. Mrs. Wood struggles, like Mom and my old summer family, just on a different level. Unfortunately, the finishing lines of my moral impulses are usually spiteful observations: Mrs. Wood and her husband act like strangers when they're not fighting and, go figure, they didn't even produce a cute baby. I cannot sustain empathy; there's always a fine reason neither to grant nor expect it.

I'm not soliciting empathy from anyone, not even Paula or Joan, although I'm painfully in love with a beady-eyed boy named Bruce ever since he sang Van Morrison's "Brown Eyed Girl" to me. When he saunters by my favorite park bench along the Grand Concourse, feigning surprise that I'm there, he joins me and Ira for hours, mostly reading the *Times* and sprinkling the air with criticism of me for reading novels and writing poetry. "I bet people will talk about the summer of 1965 for a long time, and you won't have the slightest idea why."

"The newspaper depresses me," I finally explain. "It's also

boring." One man after another and ads for stuff I can't buy. I'd much rather scribble about plumes of bus fumes and streams of dreams.

Bruce is eighteen and eager for senior year; he knows I'm heading into ninth grade but not the truth about my age. Because of the accelerated program, I sprinted through seventh and eighth grade in one year, which justifies aging myself with one year, to which I tacked on another year to reach the minimum age requirement for mother's helpers. Pretending I was fifteen at the interview, I maintained the lie when I first started to meet the neighborhood boys not good-looking enough to have girls following them. But finally, after determining the age at which he began to read the *Times,* I confess to Bruce that I'm not quite thirteen yet. I'd rather be thought deceptive than stupid. He telescopes me with those beautiful beady blue eyes, appearing, at first glance, outraged that I told a lie. "So, that explains it! You're tall, but you're completely flat. You're a kid. But you seem older, at least sometimes."

Still, Bruce keeps coming around, and he promises that in the fall he'll mail me the songs he finishes. Goading that I won't nail a college scholarship unless I read the *Times,* he laughs and pounds my arm when I retort that the newspaper is too expensive. I'll never understand what's amusing about being broke.

Ever since the first time I clambered by here on my way to the West Bronx, I've known a tiny part of my destiny stalled on the Grand Concourse. Bruce is a park statue that cannot be budged to where I live. All the Grand Concourse guys, including Jason, refer to my neighborhood as Zululand, even though if they bothered to visit me they'd most likely run up against white

112

guys seeking vengeance on preppies. These college-bound boys aren't ashamed at all when I call them snobs and cowards. Why do boys think it's cute when girls insult them?

Girls would never tolerate my digs. When I tell Paula she is acting like a slut, she blazes. I'm embarrassed now when I trek to the beach with her on rare sunny days off. At first I guessed her breasts were popping out because she couldn't afford a new bathing suit, but then she deliberately bought a skimpy bikini that showcased her baby-oil-slickened boobs. She pranced around Brighton Beach scouting for boys, and then she made out with them for hours. When they didn't phone, she cried that it was because of her frizzy hair and bad skin. Pretty soon even the skin on one of her breasts was red and scabby. She confessed that she let two boys kiss her nipples. One of them bit her left breast so hard it bled, and it must have gotten infected.

I don't want to be disloyal to Paula, yet I'm disgusted. I'll admit that I'm boy-crazy, too. Bruce seeps into my thoughts like humidity, wilting my resolve to engage Ira or to read, but I refuse to act crude like my Mom and Jackie. I wish I could tell Paula about how my mother's life was ruined by letting so many men nuzzle her, but aren't I glad to be alive? Aren't I glad that my sisters and brother are alive? How can I condemn my mother when we are her flesh and blood mistakes? She gave up her life so that we could live. Maybe that's enough truth for one family.

It seems telling the truth always involves betraying something or someone. When I stick to straightforward facts, such as "Paula, you are acting like a slut," her pimples turn bright red, and mascara streaks down her face. She stomps away. Paula is becoming like my sister Jackie, always disappearing with boys who talk about her big breasts as if they possess a future all their own.

I'm mocked for being flat-chested, but console myself by deciding that big boobs are a curse. Like most theories I have, that one is quickly contradicted. My mother has small tits and still got knocked up, repeatedly. Given the way Bruce treats me, I won't have to worry about that anytime soon. I'm a convenient audience for him, but I lack allure. My wish to be his girlfriend is abstract rather than urgent, which makes it easier to ignore his hints that I fix my hair, try on some makeup and do something about my buck teeth. Bouncy hair, flush cheeks and straight teeth are as inaccessible to me as the moon and the Grand Concourse.

15

BELONGING

The size of your bust doesn't seem to matter when the dropouts and high school boys in my neighborhood celebrate the beginning of the school year. They huddle in anticipation of girls turning a corner or walking past an alley, and then attack, blasting us in the chest with balloons bulging with cold water. The missiles burst on contact, plastering our blouses against skin, bras and T-shirts. Light-colored blouses wilt into transparency; bra patterns and nipple shapes and shades are exposed. Boys then follow us home rating our headlights and contours as if they are comparing cars. One day I'm called a flat tire and another I'm praised. "Here's one who's built for speed, not comfort." All the girls are supposed to be sporty vehicles the guys ride to some mysterious destination of their own choosing.

If I wear two layers under my blouse to protect my nipples from detection when they perk up in self-defense as the cold hits, I'm hot all day and create unnecessary laundry. Covering myself with my books after an attack only provokes more teasing about how there's nothing much to hide. Changing my route by taking the long way home from school is also chancy, I learn at someone else's expense.

Two girls on my block cut through buildings and across the elementary school recess yard to avoid their hair frizzing from a spritzing. Nine guys ambush them with a full body drenching, the whole time mimicking their cries and ridiculing them for thinking they could get away. When the girls complain at their school, the boys punish all of us.

Positioned on fire escapes and rooftops, they hurl not only balloons, but also tomatoes and, one horrible day, eggs. Even the balloons hurt as they plummet from a third story, thudding on our heads and necks like rocks. The boys tired of ogling breasts and were aiming for serious contact, which they finally achieve when one girl's glasses are broken by an egg. Her big brothers assemble a posse and teach those high school bullies a lesson.

The boys decide to play nicer with us. One Friday after school, a douser I recognize by his acne-ridden face greets me like a friend. He even knows my name. "Hear about the truce, Mary?" He lifts both of his arms and opens his hands as if under instruction from the police. "See, I'm not holding anything."

Walking next to me, he machine-guns instructions about how I should show up at the Shakespeare Avenue triangle park at four P.M. for a game of MM30. He assures me that a girl with my legs will have no trouble outrunning the other girls. Bumping up against my shoulder, he challenges me. "Be there. Don't be square."

I'm not about to admit to being intimidated or ignorant. Mom and Joan haven't heard of a game called MM30 either, but Mom urges me. "You spend too much time with your head in books and your nose in the air. Make friends in the neighborhood."

Soon I'm testing my legs and nerve with a bunch of white kids I've rarely nodded at but have noticed ever since we moved to Shakespeare and then up the hill to Merriam Avenue. One of the leaders, a hunk named George, snaps when I suggest including my friend Paula in the game. "No Jews allowed in our gang."

As the timekeeper, George signals when it's time for the girls to run and hide within a twelve-block area, promising the boys won't pursue us for a full ten minutes. I nudge some girls to range further, but they wave me off and continue ducking behind the library or the pillars of the Noonan Plaza, a six-building high-rise complex with an inner courtyard of broken benches and concrete sculptures. A girl named Cookie and two of her friends bolt with me at first. Cookie's fast and determined as she trills over her shoulder: "No boy will catch me without a fight." She leaves us behind.

The other two girls are impressed that I know which buildings have lobbies with clocks and unlocked entryways or back doors. One of them heads for a secret spot she has successfully used for two games. The other tucks herself into the first hiding place I identify, a pile of boxes underneath and on top of a table in the mail corridor of a big building. She's grateful, so I don't resent heading for my second choice, an alley that stretches at an incline between three of the buildings that climb the stairs from the Edward L. Grant Highway to Shakespeare Avenue.

I'm glad I finally sprung for a watch. Heart pounding, I consult it every minute, thinking much more time has elapsed. The boys have only twenty minutes to find us; after that I'm home free. From my vantage point I can scope out some of the guys at the top of the hill and scan the bottom. I'm watching the action and hiding at the same time. If someone heads down or up the alley, I'll scurry behind staircases or scramble upstairs in either of the two closest buildings. Even when eighteen minutes of this part of the game have passed, and I've stuck to my station for seven, I'm still sweating. I don't want to get caught. I don't want to get caught. From the way Cookie tore off and the other girl beamed at the secure hiding place I pointed out, I know something bad happens to those girls who don't scatter far enough.

After twenty minutes from our start time, I emerge victorious, but still wary. Figuring I'll play this game again, I conceal my location by skipping all the way down the alley and then sprinting up the stone steps carved into the hill. I bound to the top and cross the street to the park, where I'm disheartened. There are only ten kids there to applaud my great escape, and no one pays me much attention. One girl, who lives a bus ride away, is pissed that she arrived too late to play. "Stupid," she sneers, "you're supposed to get caught." Two of the tardy guys look forlorn. Two others are embarrassed they couldn't find anyone and one girl sulks because no one picked her.

Turns out that the dreaded culminating event is kissing. MM30 stands for Make-out Manhunt 30 minutes. The hide-and-seek part lasts thirty minutes and whatever happens after that is nobody's business. For the next hour sheepish couples slither back to the park or separate a block away. Lots of kids don't reappear; there are dinners waiting for them at home. After he returns, holding hands with a cute girl with big breasts,

George presides once again. He's the Master of Ceremonies of Make-out Manhunt 30 minutes. "The turnout is bigger every time. Saturday night should be a blast."

As I wander off with a vague salute to everyone, George acknowledges me. "I hear you got away this time. Comin' back tomorrow night?"

"I'm baby-sitting."

So he turns on me. "Who cares. You're a flat-chested skank anyway. Go home and wash your face."

I slump up the hill. Now realizing my hands are dirty from leaning into filth in the alley, I examine my face in a car mirror and discover stringy hair and a sooty left cheek. I imagined myself as a sleek deer scampering in the hills and hiding from hunters, but I'm a ragamuffin. Next time I play, I'll pocket a handkerchief and a compact.

I forget the mirror, of course, but when I return to the same spot two more times, I inspect where I rest my hands as diligently as I check the time. While climbing the stairs at the end of the game, I poke bobby pins into my scalp to tighten my hair behind my ears after combing it with my hands. The third time, Cookie salutes me for outsmarting the guys. "Two of them were looking for you," she warns, but when I describe my haunt, she congratulates me. "They'll never track you there."

But next time they do. After only eleven minutes, they're on me. One clinches my arms behind my back while the other one kisses my neck and then opens his mouth like a fish about to swallow. It's the guy with the pimples. When his face zooms in and blurs out of focus, I feel faint. Up close, all I can see is bubbles of pus or Clearasil.

I butt his chest with my head, wrench my arms away from his teammate, and sprint straight up the alley, hoping the park is empty. But the kids who are there wave when I run by. The twenty minutes are now up and they must think I scored again and am heading back home.

At school I bump into Cookie's friend I helped to hide, Judith, not at all surprised that she's in the lowest-level class. There's something muted and unfinished about her, something simple that's cute and odd as she sidles up to me and squeals that Cookie ratted me out.

I'm dumbfounded. "Why?"

"She wanted to test your reaction, or something like that." Her head rolls before she finishes what she has revved up to share. "Cookie would crucify me for snitching."

After that, Cookie surprises me again. She grows friendlier, inviting me to hang out with her and her friends any time. She's a deer and a ragamuffin, too. For the first time in my life, I'm exhilarated by belonging.

One Saturday I join Cookie, Judith and the other girl, Amy, in what they call *running*. First we terrorize the three Fanny Farmer stores within roaming distance of the triangle park on Shakespeare. Pretending one of us is buying a box of candy for her mother's birthday, we post ourselves in front of three towers of perfectly wrapped packages. At Cookie's whistle, we simultaneously knock over each carefully balanced display. Walloping our mouths in an Indian cry, we dash out.

I feel giddier than I have in my entire life when I prove myself to the tough girls by suggesting our next target: a huge wholesale/retail store of candy bins near the Grand Concourse. I promise shortcuts through the alleys to The Biggest Confectioner in the Bronx. Cookie is the leader; I'm the guide.

I've seen it before and I'm still astonished by the aisles of bins of peppermint, butterscotch, sour cherry drops and chocolate footballs that can be bought by the quarter-pound or more in any assortment desired. "A little of this, a little of that, a lot of that because they are the only candy my husband eats," a lady hums to her skinny friend. My friends are humming, too.

The sales ladies glare at us. They don't see customers, they see grubby, sweaty trouble. What a pleasure it is to surprise but not disappoint them.

Invisibly cupping small amounts of candy, we skip our hands from one bin to another and mix the contaminators around. Then we transfer an assortment from that bin on to the next. We are a coordinated destruction machine. It will cost those sneering ladies hours to sort out the containers.

In sync like a glee club or sisters, when we sense that the sales ladies' suspicions are mounting toward conviction, we saunter out, salivating and snorting: "There's nothing we want here."

Then, staking claim to the Grand Concourse as our territory, we seriously and politely accost men. "Excuse me, sir, I thought you'd want to know . . ." We point to the ground solemnly and say, "Your shoes are untied" to men wearing loafers or "Your slip is showing" to men wearing shoes with laces. Some of them curse; some actually look around their feet and calves until they hear us cackle; several seem to worry about our sanity. Not me. I never before felt so sane and clear with girls who aren't my sisters.

On another day Cookie and the girls she calls her posse lure me into *running* to the Chinese laundry a couple of blocks away.

I'm alarmed when they start whirling, yanking carefully folded shirts wrapped in plain brown paper off the shelves lining two walls of the tiny, steamy store. Then they stomp, splitting open the paper and dragging shirts on the floor with their feet. Screaming some imitation of Chinese followed by "Coolie" and "Ching Chong Challywock," they run out when the guy lunges at us with a broom. As he doubles over in the middle of the street, wheezing and coughing, Cookie threatens to grab his broom and whack him. Her friends jerk her away.

They are deliriously happy and ready to proceed to the next Chinese laundry not far away. When I head in a different direction, claiming that I have to take care of my younger siblings, Cookie grimaces. "Later for you, then." Rushing home, I fantasize about returning to the store to help the man clean up, turning Cookie in to the cops, and spending more time with girls at school in the honors classes.

The reality of my behavior has suddenly become clear: appalling cruelty that could have netted me a deserved J.D. card. The snooty ladies in the candy store had snubbed me when I first went there with pocket money from baby-sitting, but we dished out more comeuppance than they deserved. Friendship and the giddiness of revenge had enclosed me in a fog of fun that made it somehow acceptable to heckle strangers on the street. Just as I have sublime moods, I am capable of reckless, random insolence. In the right company, my spiteful streak colors my personality. I'm as mixed up as those candy bins and as startled as our targets.

16

THIGH GLIDING

Life is filled with mystery. Five weeks ago he called me a skank in front of everybody, but now Gorgeous George is holding my hand. It must be because Lacey permed my hair and he heard about how sexy I looked at Orchard Beach last weekend when a bunch of kids headed out there for sunbathing. The pimple puss told everybody that in a striped bathing suit my shape was perfect and I didn't look skinny at all. Your butt is so round, from the boardwalk I thought I was looking at a beach ball, he teased.

George has asked me to crawl into the Dugout, an exclusive space under the Edward L. Grant Highway that serves as a boys' clubhouse. When a girl named Donna showed up uninvited, they slapped her around, ripped her clothes and threw her out of the gang.

At first I'm as excited about finally seeing the Dugout as I am about George paying attention to me. A long rope ladder drops down into a dark, dirt pit, where shadows are making out on blankets. Then I'm shushed for asking how the dirt walls stay in place, but my fears demand a hearing. George orders me to shut up and kiss him in the same tone of voice with which he called me a skank, and I become even more fidgety about suffocating or suffering Donna's fate. I'm hoping a movie matron will magically appear, disapprovingly shining a flashlight on the writhing shapes.

When I wander toward the rope, George surprises me by apologizing. "It's too crowded down here. We should stay selective," he purrs while rising into the light with me. I am startled by the sun and don't care about George at all, but I can't shake him. And then I don't want to. He nibbles my neck and lips and flatters me: "You're stronger than I thought." My insides dart and swish with our tongues. Standing up kissing in the sun melts my reserve and loosens my shoulders and neck. Like a sleepwalker, I let him lead me back down into the darkness.

I am alert in this dream. Now I know why I've become boy-crazy. It's thrilling to lock lips and still keep your secrets. When George pokes at my zipper, I threaten to leave, but he entices me to relax, just relax, his soft voice hypnotizing me, his hands pushing me to the ground. I straddle and glide on his thigh and discover that I can rub against the seam of his jeans to increase the sense of ascending and descending and ascending to a sustained tickle, until suddenly everything settles. I've adjusted to the darkness and am now delighted to be flooded with the heady lightness and giggles of knowing I've finally made out with someone.

But then George heaves me off and a rock lodges in my back. "What the hell are you doing?" He looks like he wants to take a swing at me. "What kind of girl are you?"

I guess my grip on his thigh surprised him as much as me. Up close and angry, he's ugly. I'm relieved when, instead of blocking my departure, he burrows his butt farther down into the dirt and curses. "Fuck, fuck, what a waste of time."

Let him stew, I think. I'm so happy, I run all the way home, an internal wind catapulting me uphill. Suddenly, I'm starving.

The next morning, Cookie pounds on our door early enough for Mom to feel justified in yelling, which she never does in front of friends now that she's sober. Cookie, surprisingly polite, nods with deference. "I'm sorry, Mrs. Childers, but it's important."

It sure is. Overnight someone scrawled in chalk all over our door and the front steps MARY IS A WHORE. Cookie spotted the steps when she was out walking her German shepherd, whose barking attracts a neighbor in robe and curlers to her door: "Vat's de madder?" Before I know it, the neighbor galvanizes her two daughters to help us clean up even though I can tell she doesn't believe my "I didn't do anything." She only warns, "You're a smart girl. Don't blow it like your mother did, you hear me?"

I learn from Cookie that the gang will soon decide if I'm still in. Her concern about my membership in this pretend gang perplexes me. After the attack on the Chinese laundry, our friendship had soured. She taunted me that we "oughta go out *running* again," and I resisted, fearing we would escalate to more serious crimes, just like people who progress from weed to smack. But now that I'm in trouble, she's joined my rescue team.

Pissing off George is a serious matter, I'm warned by his deputy Noel, who stops by later that day. "We voted to have you stay in because you talk so good you give us class, but you gotta be careful for a while." He's as serious as one of those newsreel Nazis I've seen in history class.

Tasting something like sour milk, I reply without thinking, "You know what, I don't want to be part of this stupid gang anymore."

Sometimes hidden truth erupts under pressure. George did me a favor; he made me realize I don't need to belong with these kids I've been getting to know for the past couple of months. "For every Jew that moves out, five Spics move in," they preached. Paula had wanted me to ask my new friends, if they need Jewish kids to stay, why do they rough them up and drop their yarmulkes in mailboxes "as warmup for Saturday night"? It takes me time, but I figure out that some of them pick fights with black and Puerto Rican kids who are minding their own business. Many of the guys don't go to school, they force girls to put out, and they are mean, I now realize, ashamed of myself. Making fun and making out were the only pleasures we pursued together. I rolled in laughter when I should have been racked with guilt. How could I have forgotten the priest who thundered that it was ordinary churchgoing people who cooked dinner while neighbors were shipped off to concentration camps? It's disconcerting that my values are as disposable as a tissue. How could I have let myself be lassoed into that herd?

My time with George, Cookie and the rest in the triangle park wasn't all bad. We danced and sang to the music that crackled out of the transistor radios balanced on the balding patches of grass or plopped down on one bench after another, scrutinizing and altering heart-shaped carvings. Staring uphill in a Motown-fueled daze, I preferred the bench that was sited to view the grand entrance to the Sacred Heart Church and the hill that slants toward the Noonan Plaza, whose rooftops offer the most panoramic neighborhood view of the Hudson River. My pleasure was only occasionally ruined by the boys making noises when they glimpsed nonwhites ascending the hill that slants in a perpendicular away from the stairs that descend to a different section of the highway. They resented the minorities who occupied the few buildings across the highway that hadn't been reduced to rubble, as if blacks and Puerto Ricans stood between us and the wealth on the Grand Concourse.

I wish my social studies teacher would verify what the old Irish guy told me and Paula about these crowded hills belonging to the Appalachian Mountains. But during the geography unit we only memorized and pierced with pushpins the map locations of natural resources and capitals in Africa, Asia and Central and South America, as if preparing for lifetimes of exile or plunder.

17

LESSONS

Even here in the Bronx we imitate westerns. On Saturday night when I was out Cookie left a message with Jackie that her posse was meeting me Sunday for a lesson I'd never learn in school. They show up Sunday morning just as promised, making it impossible for me to avoid the showdown.

"There are some things in life you just have to get through," Jackie philosophizes. She's reconciled to the school of hard knocks.

We troop across the street to the basketball court, where kids have already formed a circle, knowing there's safety in numbers in the park. A fight is like a parade; it draws people out of their houses into the street. Boys and men stop shooting hoop in return for some other entertainment, this time a girl fight.

Some of my old friends from the gang shout encouragement and warnings to me: "Go down fast and cover your head" and

"Punch first and keep your fists tight the whole time." Joan stands there crying.

Before banging on me, Cookie starts howling, working herself up. "We're all sick of being snubbed by you. You think you're better than anybody else."

Don't they remember they were the ones who threatened to kick me out?

Her posse chants, "Miss Posture, Miss Posture," the same way they do when I walk past them, always on the other side of the street. Years of practicing walking with books on my head so that I can impress adults with money have trained me to walk straight and stiff. It's maddening that a requirement in one environment is an offense in another. How will I develop character if the world requires me to be a chameleon?

"You never stop to talk to people. You and your plaid pleated skirts swing by like you're heading someplace better," Cookie yells at me, now bouncing on her feet and pumping her fists like a fighter. She has practiced her speech as much as her moves.

Trying not to lose face by showing fear, I breathe deeply to steady my voice, holding on to my persistent but usually futile hope that rationality is contagious: "Why would I stop and talk to people who yell 'Miss Posture' at me when I walk by?"

Then she's coming at me, furious: "Snob!" "Bitch!"

Our battle ends quickly. I manage to punch her feebly half the number of times she punches me and then to trip her with the move I used to watch Lacey pull on Jackie. Although I hear Jackie cheer me on with "Kick her in the face while she's down," I'm thinking more along the lines of splitting. But Cookie is too fast for me. She pulls me down on top of her and then rolls me over as if I'm nothing more than a rag doll.

She's so strong, I wonder if she's a dyke. There's something peculiar about her gaze when she pins me down and spits on my face. "It's a good thing you didn't kick me, or I would have killed you," she shouts for the benefit of everyone. And then she lets me up.

I walk away shaking, but still straight and stiff, with Gorgeous George at my side, pretending to be my escort or promoter: "You did good."

Joan reports the verdict on the streets: I landed a few strong punches, but Cookie won, as expected. Maybe I'll know enough to treat her with respect in the future.

Now I add three blocks to my walk down the hill to avoid Cookie and her posse. They are dangerous, Joan tells me; they have a reputation all over the Bronx for yanking open the earlobes of Puerto Rican girls. Joan knows about it from one of her friends whose mother outlawed dangling earrings.

It's a good thing I seized the opportunity to leave that crowd in a dignified huff. Walking around, my eyes on the horizon, I recognize that Cookie was right: I needed to learn a lesson. Trouble is, I can't remember lessons when there's no one I trust as a source of knowledge.

For years Mom has tried to inflict on me a message similar to Cookie's. People who speak well and read widely may be admirable, but if you stand out, you'll be picked out. You're inviting trouble and loneliness when you distinguish yourself from your own by choosing to care about good grades, books, accents and magazine clothes. Even though Mom's warnings and punishments increased my determination at times, I have to give her credit. Against my will, I've absorbed resentment and the nagging perception that my ambitions are disloyal, and worse, punishable.

Mom likes Paula just fine but objects to the Bronx High School of Science, where I want to go, because it's too Jewish. When I challenge her, she retaliates. "Most people get too full of themselves when they are told they are smarter than other people," Mom informs my sisters to nods of approval. "That's why kids down the block turned on Mary. She goes to that school and she'll start using even bigger words and holding her nose in the air." Even in a good mood, she still firmly vetoes the idea of a special high school: "Honey, how you going to come up with enough money for transportation and for the clothes that will keep those kids from making fun of you?" There's no persuading her. If I try to fly too high, she'll singe my Icarus wings.

Paula's mom offers to explain that if I score high enough I deserve the rare opportunity offered by the Bronx High School of Science, but she'd better not because my mother will yell at her and not let me sleep over anymore. I'm afraid that if we bug Mom, she'll condemn Joan to the vocational track. She's already announced that she won't permit Joan to enroll in the accelerated junior high school program that ruined me. Mom knows that I'm moving out of this house and this neighborhood as soon as I graduate from high school, which is going to be when I'm sixteen at this rate, and she isn't about to lose Joan that fast.

Joan agrees with Mom that there's no reason for people to leap over friends the same age. I wish someone had talked to me about self-presentation and grades when I was in sixth grade, but my

131

coaching annoys the sister who used to rely on me. She scoffs at me for the way I study *Seventeen* as if it is the periodic table, memorizing which elements complement the largest number of alternatives, instructing her on wardrobe as if I've concocted a secret formula for success. Joan doesn't want to contemplate teachers judging us for how we dress or recognize that her opportunities in life drop in tandem with her grades.

She used to remind me of Shirley Temple, the wide-eyed little curly-headed girl who deserved to be America's favorite child star. But the curious girl has gone into hiding and been replaced by someone who exits conversations chanting, "Don't care, don't care." Ever since three black girls beat her up and made her turn over money every day for weeks, she has shirked the battle to do better. Joan still reads, but she also stays up late glued to the TV, skips school and spends hours playing cards and board games with Alice and Ralph.

Mom periodically grants Joan the opportunity to bask in the sun of her approval: "Joan is naturally contented with what she has, which is more than I can say for some people. She's a blessing for me, I'll tell you that. I couldn't earn a dime if she wasn't so good with Alice, Ralph and Emma."

When I watch eleven-year-old Joan trudge up the hill from the library, with seven-year-old Alice and five-year-old Ralph flanking her rear, I behold troops transporting their reinforcements. If they borrow six books, the maximum allowed out at one time, neither Alice nor Ralph can see where they are walking; they just track Joan's shadow and determination. They often return with *Junior Scholastic*, books about cowboys, and picture books to show Emma. Ralph aches for his very own books on magic tricks, but we're afraid he'll hurt himself or set the apartment on fire again. So he scours the library and comes home with strange finds about subjects like alchemy and vivisection.

Alice frequently misplaces barrettes and socks, but she carefully deposits her plasticized library card in one sacred place from which it can be retrieved at a moment's notice. That card has been her passport to sophistication from the first day Mom marched her to the library, making a big to-do about it. We all get our chance to be like the girl in *A Tree Grows in Brooklyn*.

Mom still discourages school attendance, but has changed her tune about library books. Now she boasts: "All of my kids except Jackie are readers. They'd choose the library over a candy store."

When I'm in my spiteful mood, I think Mom needs to be the only one around with a high school diploma. She rarely objected to Jackie skipping school and then dropping out and now she's encouraging Jackie's engagement to Martin, a quiet, good-looking apprentice in the longshoremen's union. "How else will Jackie afford her own place?" Mom asks. Showing up late and fighting with co-workers, Jackie at seventeen is no more suited for work than school.

We all know Martin is a rebound boyfriend from Bad News; too quiet for Jackie, I think, when I observe her trying to rouse him from a chair where he sits for hours, not even twiddling his thumbs. "What about a GED before you get married, Jackie?" I ask in what Mom sarcastically calls my "infinite wisdom."

"You don't need a GED to raise babies," Martin replies while Mom nods. He probably doesn't want her to have a high school degree just because he doesn't.

I live in a place where, for better and for worse, tender and tense togetherness matters more than individual accomplishment and effort. On days when varicose veins bring her to tears, everyone takes turns massaging Mom's legs. To decline to participate because you have math homework is an unforgivable act of betrayal. "My legs are bursting with grape Kool-Aid" is the way Mom explains the streaks of purple that prevent her from waitressing the way she used to before she got pregnant again. All she can do now is perch on a stool behind a cash register or counter. We're losing money at a time when we need more of it.

I often think of what Rico from the bodega on Webster Avenue used to say to any kid who wandered into the store: "You can't get good jobs until you've proven you can handle bad jobs. No guarantees, no matter what anyone tells you. But there's no chance if you don't try." Another time he preached at a whole family. "That's what's there for people like us. You want to visit your people on the Island, you want to go home to the Island to die, you work hard." He's the one who taught me that if you skip school, you're learning to skip work. If you don't learn to work, you'll always be beholden to someone. I yearn to earn.

Mom accepts work that comes her way, but she doesn't hustle for opportunities. Even worse, she poisons the kids with contaminated information: "There's nothing to look for"; "All good things come to those who wait"; and "No matter what you do, you can't get ahead." When she stands in my way, I try to forgive her now that I've figured out she forswears upward mobility out of fear we will leave her behind or break our hearts failing.

On the day that I learn I missed the cut for the Bronx High School of Science, Mom touts the rejection as a sign that she was right: hankering to go where you don't belong backfires. Her warnings crawl under my skin: Maybe I shouldn't strive for anything I'm unlikely to achieve. Losing hurts. Maybe it's easier to earn money than good grades and test scores.

18

CARNIVAL SECRETS

I'm looking forward to finishing junior high school in two months. But I keep wondering, have I really graduated if I don't attend the graduation ceremony? I dream of a grand entrance made possible by my father dishing out the money I need for fees and clothes.

When a neighbor first whispered that my father's carnival was scheduled for Brooklyn and he wanted to reunite with me without Mom knowing, I started to shake. Then, on the way to see him, the lurching train sounded distinctly like "I'm sorry, I'm sorry," but I didn't know who was apologizing. I've always expected him to show up again, handsome, wealthy and finally able to rescue us. Instead, I'm sneaking around, prickled by questions: How long has he known where we live? How many neighbors have seen him? My heart seizes when I think that for the past six years he has roamed in and out of New York without so much as a hello.

The carnival is smellier and more insidious than I remember it. When I was a kid, the games and rides distracted my attention from the Adults Only tents. From the looks of those who drunkenly crawl in and out and from snippets of conversation I overhear, I now know that sex and card games are for sale inside. Were gambling and prostitution the reason for Dad's short stint in prison, or was it because of his concession con?

Even though he spirited me here, Dad hugs me hello, dutifully exchanges a few sentences, and then leaves me in charge of bilking chump change from his occasional customers. Most people pass by my booth because they want to toss or shoot instead of selecting a rubber duck floating in a small pond of plastic lily pads, hoping that the number on the duck's ass matches the number of one of the grand prizes displayed on the back wall. Nothing else to do, I inspect every single bottom, finally figuring out that the basketballs and huge stuffed animals lack corresponding numbers in the pond. Folks don't have a chance of winning more than a pencil, a pinwheel or a balloon.

During one of two stretches when Dad breezes back, I express my outrage at the scam and threaten to refer to him forever after as My Dad Donald the Dirty Duck Dealer. He laughs at his new title, but when I explain alliteration to him he scolds me that I should never call people illiterate.

My father's surprising re-entry into my life crashes through a hemisphere of hope that had sheltered me for years. When I complain that Mom constantly screams, he preaches that she is a good woman and deserves my respect no matter what she does. He's one to talk. I want to stab him with my questions. "You used to say that being common-law man and wife was as good as getting married, then how come it was so easy for you to leave?" Ignoring my question, he recites for the hundredth time their first encounter. He first glimpsed Sandy when he was a pin setter, before bowling alleys automated; it was love at first blink. I refuse to laugh at the old joke about both of them having glass eyes. That's all they ever had in common.

Our carnival reunion becomes a tug-of-war. I'm not on his side anymore. Mom would never disappear for six years and then make me work instead of spending time together. Unlike him, she doesn't reek of booze anymore. She might ignore my questions, but she would never delay this long to ask about school.

When he finally asks, I jump at my chance. I blather that there's no way I'll attend graduation in a secondhand dress, so I just won't be able to pick up my awards. I've saved enough to cover the shoes, bag and fees, but a fancy dress with no other use would wipe me out. My Dad Donald the Dirty Duck Dealer promises me the big prize: he'll send me the twenty bucks I need if I vow not to tell anyone about him blowing in and out of town. Before splitting again, he pats me on the head: "I bet you're happy now, Monkey."

My Dad and I always had secrets. I was his firstborn, so everyone agreed that it made sense that he baptized me, and only me, with nicknames. To him, I was Little Phil, or Punk, or Monkey. When my mother fussed about me contracting the sniffles, he would remind her that the punk was so healthy the rain could do nothing to her. With his blessing, I rarely caught colds.

When he still lived with us, one day I saw him grinning at me as I climbed up a street pole and slid down again. Mom would have forced me down, yelling that my arms wouldn't hold me, I'd fall and crack open my skull and she'd have to rush me to the hospital. But he grinned, so I kept climbing and sliding until tired enough to stand contentedly next to him.

"You little monkey," he said, "what are you doin'?"

I spoke up to my good-looking father through an echo chamber: "It feels good between my legs."

I waited for him to yell, but he patted me on my head. "Don't let anyone ever tell you that what feels good is bad." He swung my arm a couple of times as we walked home together. I know he didn't breathe a word to Mom.

Our secrets used to be pearls I cherished as proof that I was special to him, but now they are little dried turds a cat wouldn't bother to bury. Two weeks pass, then three. Mom wonders why the sudden interest in the mail. I had lied to everyone about where I disappeared to until two A.M. that Saturday, so maybe it's fair that he conned me.

How could I have believed Dad the Cad? I time myself for a half hour literally kicking my own butt, running down the street pumping my legs back high enough for them to bang my bottom cheeks. My knees hurt. I'm a human pogo stick; even my emotions bounce up and down. I care, I don't care, I care, I don't care, I don't care.

When he first disappeared, I informed people who hadn't even asked that my father was a Traveling Accountant, assigned against his wishes to a southern territory. I had refined the concept of Traveling Salesmen to escape the jokes that compromised the dignity of that particular profession. When adults looked at me pityingly because my father worked far away, I stiffened with contempt for them for falling for my lie. Then I had contempt for myself in the middle of a baby-sitting interview when one lady grabbed me in an eye-lock: "There's no need to lie to me about your father."

After that, I no longer advertised him as a Traveling Accountant. He briefly entered my waking dreams as a hill dweller. Next, my mind cleverly merged his disappearance with the assassination of JFK in 1963. Death is a man's tightest alibi for not showing up. Eclipsed over time, my father darkened into an ennobled silhouette stitched inside me. He left no traceable footprints, only a rich, dark soil in which my yearning for something unnamed grew. Then he unsettled my psyche by disappointing me all over again.

When I start high school in September 1966, I won't tolerate nicknames. My name is Mary, Mary, not Monkey, not Punk, not Hairy Mary, not Scary Mary. Mary, one of Sandy's kids. The one who shuns graduation ceremonies. The one who starts tenth grade at the age of thirteen and wants more than anything to graduate at the official dropout age, sixteen. Using the techniques for lettering and drawing straight lines I learned in art class to create my own calendar, I mark off day after day in my march toward freedom. I prize my father's one enduring gift: the ability to leave no matter how much others cleave.

19

MALCOLM X
AND THE SCARLET A

Now that I've moved on to a better job than taking care of Ira, I plan on buying my own clothes for my next graduation. Every day after school I hop two buses to Washington Heights, a northern section of Manhattan, on the other side of the Harlem River from the West Bronx. At three P.M. I wait outside a Muslim school for Robert Williams, a hefty eight-year-old black kid. I drag him back to his neighborhood, prepare a snack, and hound him into finishing his homework before *Gilligan's Island* and his mother's return from work.

This is the best job I've had so far. I couldn't believe my eyes when I skimmed the classified section in the *Times:* "Baby-sitter for active boy, M-F, 3–6:30pm, three blocks east of Grand Concourse, $15 wk." This is why you have to read the want ads every single week, no matter how slim the pickin's. Every once in a while, there's a gem. This job pays as much as baby-sitting for Ira, with one-third the required hours.

The interview was another surprise. Practicing my best posture, I walked into a big dining room filled with black people: Miss Williams, her mom and dad, her best friend, and Robert. They let me know it was about time white people started taking care of black children, but they didn't want no racist and I looked awfully young.

I look older when I start talking, so I quickly repeated the lie about my age in my letter of application and proved that I wasn't a racist by identifying Martin Luther King, Jr., as my hero. This was my first opportunity to say such a thing, and I immediately embraced it as true. I've listened to him reverentially whenever Mom has approvingly crooked her finger at the television or sighed, "This man is righteous," after reading quotations from one of his speeches.

Robert challenged me, to the great pride of his mother and grandmother, "Why would a white person make the King a hero?" They all smiled when I said he advocated for all poor people and for an America that was better than the slave past.

Then I described my baby-sitting experience, at home and for others. "What kind of work yo' father do with all these kids?" Miss Williams's mom asked, and I didn't skip a beat: "My dad left years ago. It's my mom who works, but mostly she relies on welfare."

Miss Williams quizzed me: "You're on welfare? You wrote that letter of application yourself?"

"I write well, and I can assist your son with his schoolwork," I assured her.

142

Miss Williams's father, so formal I thought he must have once been a train porter, explained they needed to confer for a minute and I should help myself to some of those cookies. I sat there munching on cookies and that word *confer,* head tilted to read titles on the row of books to my right. The spotless apartment sparkled with colorful posters and fabrics.

When they came back, Miss Williams offered me the job on the condition that I never call her ma'am again, and then she grinned. She is beautiful and gracious; that's why she can be a receptionist at a television studio in Manhattan. But because she has a college degree in biology from Howard University in Washington, D.C., she expected a better job. "I wish someone had told me black girls can't land jobs in labs," she told me, as though I was the one who didn't keep her informed. Getting pregnant ended her dreams of medical school; Robert's dad splitting kept her from ever getting ahead. But rather than stiffing someone else, Sandra Williams offered me the fair wage she hasn't yet received.

The multiple shifts in my overcrowded high school oblige most of the white kids to start classes at seven A.M. and finish at noon. Instead of dawdling with others, I steal time for homework while journeying to pick up my charge and barrel through the rest while pressuring him to do the same. I double-check his homework more than my own. Once Robert realizes he can make twenty-five cents from each of his friends who wants to kiss the white girl on the cheek, he becomes cooperative, and we settle into a rhythm that works for both of us.

Less so for his mom. Every day we meet her at the train so I can take off and he can badger her for more treats when they pass the grocery store. Miss Williams never enjoys a moment's peace, not even a chance to walk in solitude from the El three blocks to her apartment.

To protect myself, I suppress the temptation to allow her more time for herself. The later it gets, the more I cower during the eleven-block walk home. After dark, kids pull fire alarms or set fires in garbage cans, wait for the firemen to arrive, and then fling Coke bottles at them. Simon and Garfunkel should be singing about The Sounds of Sirens. My mom says that the whole city is suffering because so many black and Puerto Rican kids are being egged on by irresponsible adults. Then the police make things worse by protecting the racist bastards who are itching for chances to swing billy clubs at black children. You have to be prepared to duck and run if violence erupts or if you are bombarded by slogans about who is right, who is wrong and what will make a difference.

Darwin's survival of the fittest, which I learn about in tenth-grade biology, is a revelation to me. When I mention to Miss Williams my convictions about evolution, hoping to impress her, she being a biology major and all, she doesn't yell at me for having an unchristian notion the way Mom did. Miss Williams harshly hands me a copy of *The Autobiography of Malcolm X*: "Black people have always known that's how white people think."

I don't know how I think, but I know I'm white. I read the book in small doses, with my increasingly anemic, rushed attention. Is this what all those little black kids are learning at that Muslim school? You have to hate whitey to survive, Miss Williams says, smiling warmly at me. It's sort of like boys who flirt by making fun of girls.

Before I return the book, when I take Robert home one day I discover his mother waiting in her pajamas with her hair in corkscrews. The house is a mess. I eye chunks of glass shattered on the floor, reflecting back the shelves of books and Black Power posters on the wall. Gasping "You've been broken into!" I move toward her, but she yells at me. "My boyfriend beat me up and trashed the house. I bet you think I'm a nigger now." I'm hurt by her yelling at me, but mostly I feel for her pain and shame.

Instead of crying, I summon my less timid self. "Miss Williams, I don't think of anyone as a nigger, but especially you. You are the most disciplined and"—I search for a word—"well-groomed woman I have ever met. My mother picks much worse boyfriends than you do I bet. And you stopped at one kid."

I didn't even know how much I admired Miss Williams until I called her well groomed, but the word makes her laugh at me, gently. She dismisses me for the next two days, but pays for a full week anyway. My mom would be generous like this if she held a real job.

After I wrangle from Robert a promise not to bug his mother, he lets me hug him for the first time in weeks. "I'll take care of her, I promise," this impressive child says with a solemnity that is part of Muslim schooling I have come to respect. Muslims advise black people not to destroy their own neighborhoods, and I suspect they have every right to scorn white people. Even me.

Although it's true that I never think of anyone as a nigger, I do on occasion flicker with the insult "Black Fool." I'm ashamed of being white and of my fear while walking home through an almost completely black neighborhood.

My favorite strategy for curtailing catastrophic imaginings

while walking home is to mentally count the cash I'm accumulating. Two more weeks in this job, and I'll escape my debt to the dentist. Knowing welfare doesn't reimburse root canals, he offered to save my tooth for only forty dollars. He said it was good for the character of people like me to grow accustomed to buying services. He doesn't seem to know that most of us would buy more if we could earn more. I wanted to bellow, hand on hip and attitude in my voice, in admiring imitation of certain ladies, *Sir, you've been brainwashed by stories about people hopping into Cadillacs after cashing government checks. Most of the people on welfare I know can't drive and react to a ride as if it's a grand vacation.* But I didn't want him to withdraw his offer of a reduced rate, and in a darkened corridor of my conscience I knew what he was referring to.

Mom's always crying that welfare doesn't "pay" enough, as if it's a job. She's losing her will to earn money and resents any reminder that other folks work hard to support people like us. Since no man has delivered on his part of the deal, sometimes her attitude toward the government is "I made the babies; the Man should pay the bills." Her withered face and bent body perhaps justify the way she sleeps through the morning even though she no longer drinks. But I can't come up with an excuse for the younger people in my neighborhood who party at night, ignore their kids during the day and treat welfare like a trust fund.

Not that finding and keeping work is easy. On top of school, budgeting and shopping are chores in themselves. When other kids refer to catching up on snooze time until midafternoon on a Saturday, I'm jealous of their leisure. It's hard to tell what's wearing me down more: the envy or the lack of sleep. Collecting cash and paying bills yield concrete results, but they don't compensate for the lack of freedom. I live by the clock and miss the dream time in which curiosity and imagination flourish.

Every once in a while reading for school is still a precious experience. Rereading a paragraph can be soothing. But most of the time my schoolwork is something I rush through, dreading the teacher's response. Anything less than a B or an 80 endangers my future. Publicly praised by a teacher, I blush with vindication. I feel the same way I felt in elementary school. In grades four through six, I scribbled little reports about the supplementary readings and produced lists of new words gleaned from the pages I sped through. I noticed next to nothing but unconnected words. On my quest for extra credit, motivated by speed instead of content, I acquired bad reading habits along with my extended vocabulary list.

There's no point in striving to be a straight-A student anymore. Enthusiasm about grades or ideas is a magnet for mockery. Even Joan avoids me if I get excited about school. When I came home with an A for my midterm history paper, she told me she was sick of my boasting. Mr. Levine had pulled me aside to say he had a special assignment for me and one other student in the class who always aced the tests. Instead of the standard take-home essay exam, we could choose to answer ten questions about one of five books. This is what is great about high school honors, I discovered: we are given the honor of choosing. I chose R. H. Tawney's *Religion and the Rise of Capitalism*. It is one of the best books I have ever read because it explains connections between work and religion and makes the past come alive. I sulked when Mom and Joan refused to read Mr. Levine's praise of how well I understood the book.

Mom said, "You think every book you read in that damned honors program is the best book you've ever read, like you just discovered your own belly button." When I protested, she made my sisters and brother giggle by putting her hands on her hips and imitating my voice, "I hope none of you turns out like your know-it-all sister."

I try to say nothing, nothing. I gag on aspirations as I swallow my words.

20

MACE

After I give up on making friends in my neighborhood, I occasionally slither into overheard conversations at school, embarrassing everyone with such practiced lines as "I've never been to a sweet sixteen party," and "What are those dances like?"

Finally a girl named Rochelle hands me an invitation to her birthday celebration, kindly explaining she would have mailed it weeks before if she had my address. At her party she dangles my paltry gift of a clearance brown cardigan in befuddlement before discarding it on the gift table. But she's still friendly to me after that, suggesting we study Spanish together and inviting me to a dance at the YMHA, the Young Man's Hebrew Association.

I can dance, but I can't converse. I spend the night grasping for a topic of conversation that will make me as beguiling as those who carelessly chat about family vacations, record albums and Greenwich Village boutiques. Questions about what my father does for a living reduce me to silence until I deploy my standard strategy for escaping social discomfort with classmates—picking on someone else. When Rochelle is complimented for the pop art jumper she bought in the Village, I point out you can buy the exact same item at Lerner's, a low-cost chain, for much less. In genuine distress she insists that couldn't possibly be the case and, frothing with spite, I tease her for being a princess. She's never again seen in the jumper or with me. Following the dance, I spurn a dribble of invitations from classmates. Offensive rejection is my primary social gambit.

Then my luck revives. Just as Paula flits away in the arms of an older man, I meet a lanky girl named Carol who proudly introduces herself as a Polak when we are the only ones in history class on a Jewish holiday. More quietly she reveals that she recently transferred from a Catholic high school because her father took off. She's squeezing two honors classes into her commercial schedule and plans on becoming an executive secretary, like her mother. When Carol invites me to a dance at the CYO, the Catholic Youth Organization, she loans me accessories.

Soon I ride a magic carpet into a social life with boys who mostly talk about sports but are never gruff and gross. Boys like these are potions, not people. If I absorb one into my life, I'll be transformed. Carol and I, along with her friend Ann, bond as accomplices plotting escape from our mothers' fate with men. We refuse to be like Ann's mom; she sells evening clothes but hasn't dressed up since her husband split over a decade ago.

On a tip from Carol, as soon as I turn fourteen and qualify for special working papers, I pick up a Saturday job folding and straightening racks of clothes at B. Altman's on Fifth Avenue in

Manhattan. It's the type of place where men in suits read newspapers in comfortable stuffed chairs while their wives shop for clothing that is too pricey for me even on clearance and with an employee discount.

This gig pays $1.70 an hour, considerably more than taking care of Robert, but it costs to take the train and dress appropriately. When I'm offered Christmas rush hours that overlap with my Robert routine, I'm stumped. How should I balance short-term opportunity, long-term obligation and my amplified list of needs?

In late November, digging a paper clip into my cuticles to pierce through my anxiety, I confess my dilemma to Miss Williams. "If I earn this extra money, I can afford root canals to save the two teeth that are killing me. Otherwise, they have to be removed. All my teeth will grow in different directions."

I should remember that she is a calm college graduate with only one kid testing her sanity. She oozes southern comfort today. "Too bad you can't afford braces, girl." And then she solves my problem: "Robert is visiting Georgia most of the holiday. I trust you to identify a reliable substitute for the three remaining weeks of school."

I have just the person, Lori, a black girl in my building who wants to buy her boyfriend a Christmas present. Why she'd buy a present for a guy who's always late is a mystery to me, but I'll take advantage of it. Lori's too busy with her man for job hunting, but is game when I turn Robert over to her at half my pay. Her parents forbid her to cross over the University Heights Bridge by bus to pick him up, but they allow her to meet me at his house. Each day she bustles in, proud of holding her first job, and I hustle out to arrive in Manhattan by five P.M. Lori envies my freedom, so I make the mistake of divulging to her the oxymoron I heard that captures my situation: benign neglect. Once she expresses sympathy that I'm neglected, I vow to keep my collection of oxymorons to myself.

Oxymorons, paradoxes, ironies and ambiguities help me embrace the sharp contrasts in my life. There's trash in the gutters in my neighborhood and in Robert's. Sometimes landlords don't replace windows in vacant apartments. Cracked, empty clay pots on windowsills testify to the lingering ghosts of plant life. Many of the cars permanently parked against a slice of curb sport an ensemble of two or three hubcaps, chipped windshields and doors that clash with the rest of the car.

My house isn't much better. Cats and one kid after another have idly carved and scratched into the upholstered sofa and chairs to scrape the wood underneath. There's a perennial film of smoke hovering in the kitchen and living room from Mom's and Jackie's cigarettes. If a light switch stops working, it's never fixed. We cautiously step around extension cords looped through the apartment just as we dodge the trash strewn through the streets.

Then I sail into the glistening, pristine Trim the Tree Shop at B. Altman's, where I am surrounded by voluminous display trees colorfully blinking on and off. The Christmas shop sells expensive ornaments from around the world: angels hand-stitched from triangles of velvet, transparent emerald green glass bulbs, and tiny, jewel-studded musical instruments and farm animals.

I watch people quickly scan all five of the sample decorated trees and then order an entire setup delivered to their houses for a phenomenal price. They are usually divorced fathers who don't have the time or interest to scrupulously select one item after another. I wonder if their kids have ever sniffed and poked among balsam, hemlock and pine trees bundled against buildings by guys who have driven down from Canada. Each year, selecting a tree from a street market and hauling it home with Mom has given me and my siblings our one and only taste of being frontiersmen. I can't picture these men helping kids string tinsel and lights or balancing on a chair poking an angel upright.

Facing the sparkling bathroom mirror at Altman's, I imitate the voices and gestures of genteel people who pick whatever they want without looking at the price, but aren't show-offs. One lady mused that she is compelled to visit the shop every Christmas season because it's where both of her grandparents purchased their holiday decorations. She exuded the aura of family wealth and continuity.

Eager to remain in favor with my supervisor, I stepped out of my role only once. After fondling a tasseled red satin bell, a customer leaned toward her friend regretfully: "I shouldn't spend eleven dollars on one ornament, I know I shouldn't." Intending to be helpful, I directed her to another store where it sells for three dollars less. Without thanking me, she hurried away in embarrassment rather than relief about the prospect of saving money. Turns out there's a reason to stick to the script; ad-libbing disconcerts the customers.

I can compare our prices with those at Saks Fifth Avenue because that's where Ann works. She and Carol and I decided to work in different stores to share discounts. Carol chose Macy's. When our quitting hours overlap, we ride the train home together, but they bail out two stops before me to switch trains on the way to their nicer neighborhood.

When they leave, I bury my head in schoolbooks while tapping my antenna for signals of danger. Gangs of girls might attack me or men could stalk me through the long blocks between the train station and where I live. The Catholic Church taught me to be vigilant about sin, but I'm mostly concerned about crime.

I cultivate a particular look for my train ride. Instead of stretching my lips as much as possible over my buck teeth, as I normally do, I deliberately stick out my teeth, an intent gesture that I sustain only by also slightly crossing my eyes. Bangs swept off my forehead, I flaunt my bushy eyebrows. They are connected with so much hair on the bridge of my nose that at a quick glance they look like one overarching brow, my crown of thorns.

Betting that only pretty girls are raped, I enjoy controlling the exact degree of my ugliness. When kids on the train mock my appearance, or more gentle people glance at me and then piteously consult their companions about whether or not I'm retarded, I feel perversely triumphant. It's just like my satisfaction when I pass for a cripple. If I drag a leg slightly behind me and hitch my body to one side, I can hobble past groups of Puerto Rican guys without them grabbing their crotches and yelling "*Mira, flaca, puta*, gimme some pussy."

But disguising my face and changing my gait won't protect me as I maneuver around the dark streets, the overpass of the highway, and the shells of buildings that resemble the Roman ruins featured in my stash of free brochures collected from Fifth Avenue travel agents. I carefully navigate the maximum distance from the places evil men may be hiding. Vacant lots and razed buildings invite aggression in men as much as the sparkle and spaciousness of Altman's elicit my hushed tone with customers.

Fiercely gripping my Mace, I recite to myself again and again what I will do if someone attacks me.

Under these conditions, I guess it's not surprising that I can't enjoy the moon and the stars I read about in poetry. The quiet I usually crave is menacing once it is dark. Yet, I splurge on the bus only if it's especially cold or raining or it happens to be there when I step off the train. Then I reproach myself for paying to ride nine blocks when I need to save for an empire-waist dress or the white midcalf boots I crave. I fear that rape may lurk in my indefinite future, but the social hostility reserved for the poorly dressed girl in the honors classes is a daily, immediate threat. I long to pass as a regular teenage girl.

I am only momentarily surprised one night when a man jumps from behind a garbage bin on the street and grabs me in a chokehold. Because he slurs his words, I couldn't follow his orders even if I wanted to. I've read that you should pinpoint an attacker's weapon before taking action, but after carrying Mace for so many weeks, I feel compelled to use it before knowing if he's armed. Primed for reaction rather than observation, I vaguely spray behind me in the direction of where I visualize his face.

When I hear him swear "Oh shit!" and feel his hold relaxing, I take off running two blocks until I can duck into the first open place I see, a bar. The men slouched over their drinks nod hello while the bartender becomes immediately solicitous. "You okay, you sure you're okay?" I repeat three times that my attacker was definitely white. When the bartender returns after scouring the street for the punk, he offers me a soda while he calls a cab. "It'll be free," he pledges, as if he can see my concern.

It's not until I'm in the cab that my shock subsides enough for other reactions to surface. I should call the police. But nothing actually happened to me. The cops never find anyone anyway. Will they confiscate my illegal spray? Suddenly the incident seems too ordinary to dwell on beyond remembering always to be prepared.

After I recount my escapade to Joan and Mom at home during the commercials, Mom cites another reason I can't file a police report. What if the cops inform welfare that I'm earning? The cheap bastards will dock her check. It's hard enough as it is.

Lacey hears about the episode from Joan and lectures me. Risking safety to hoard money for Capezio shoes on sale shows poor judgment; it's penny wise, pound foolish. Lacey's indictment sucks me down a tunnel of memory where I feel like I'll gag more than my attacker did from the Mace. Someplace, sometime, one of my mom's sleepovers whipped out a ten-dollar bill for tea bags, milk, bread, real butter and cinnamon so that we could all feast on cinnamon toast for Sunday breakfast. Halfway back home, Joan and I marveled that the cashier had returned a dollar extra. Only $1.29 more could buy a jumbo box of éclairs. We didn't think this guy, whoever he was, would mind.

We misread him. He blew up like we had stolen and crashed a brand-new car. "You thieving brats. Get in your rooms and don't come out until after everyone else has eaten."

Mom cozied up to him while reprimanding us. Of course, we should have returned the extra dollar and not spent anybody else's money. These were still her drunken days, but she stayed Sunday-morning gentle.

Not him. He lectured us on frugality and how the poor man

must guard every dollar. Squirming away from Mom's efforts to keep her head on his shoulder and an arm around his waist, he ferreted out from under the couch the wooden handle of a paddle ball set that had long been detached from its string and little red ball. He dusted it off lovingly. "You coddle your kids and they'll go bad. They need a father to take a paddle to them."

Finally Mom rose to the occasion. "Don't you dare hit my kids."

He was finished before our éclairs. With a mouth full of cream, and chocolate on her lips, Mom wished him "Good riddance" as he slammed the door. "What a miser!"

This man's force field of anger had launched lightning into my brain, frightening me into frugality, into watching every dollar just as he advised. I remember him not as a person, but as a rigid law I've never quite figured out how to obey.

Lacey is right, as usual. You have to take care of little things, like bus passes and bus fare, as well as thinking about the big stuff. Fine principles like frugality can be misapplied. Even though I want to buy Mom a fabulous present next Christmas, I'm also hopping the bus after dark from now on. If I don't save enough by Christmas, then by her birthday I'll have the cash for a sturdy shopping cart to replace the old rusted clunker she bumps and pulls over curbs and sidewalk cracks, as worn out by dirty sheets and clothes as she once was by babies. At Christmas I'll definitely have the money to surprise Ralph and Alice with the best quality paddle balls—and I'll try to have the patience to ensure they know how and when to use them.

21

SUMMER CAMP

"What have I done that the Lord is punishing me so much through my children?" Mom laments as she scrubs blood off seven-year-old Ralph's face. He stands still with his arms out so that Joan, who is also crying, can examine the belt marks. Like a tree that can withstand anything, he doesn't put his arms down until Joan coaxes and bends them toward his sides. He won't say much about what happened.

The more he withholds, the more Mom vents: "What kind of mother am I that I can't protect my kids from this?" Mom expresses what we all fear: "All hell is going to break loose on these streets one of these summer nights. It'll be worse than Watts and the 1964 Harlem riots, worse than what happened last summer when that Spanish kid was killed by a cop. How long can black people put up with what this country has done to them? How long can the cops put up with hippies and Mau Maus insulting them?"

She asks questions of the air to avoid again interrogating Ralph, who freezes if you probe for more than monosyllables. He whispers, "Black kids," and nothing more.

The fifth time Ralph crawled home at lunchtime, bruised and disheveled, refusing to return to school, Mom marched into his class and held her ground while kids in the back row jeered. Now that the right to go to school is threatened, she values it more. Ralph's teacher cringed and signaled to confer outside the classroom. In the hall she warned, "You know, you could be escalating your son's problem." My mom finally backed down when the principal explained it wasn't just a race thing. The same black kids were beating up black kids, whose parents also couldn't protect them. He wasn't about to risk a riot by making more of a fuss about a white child taking his licks. Once she returned home, it occurred to Mom to doubt that any other kid was attacked virtually every week, but she knew that her audience with the authorities was over.

Ralph sometimes mentions black classmates who give him cover or a heads-up when a book sails toward his head from the back of the room. He and a Dominican kid share comics, and there's a black girl who practices multiplication tables with anyone who is interested. Two tough white boys call him a sissy and piss on his notebooks. Still, it's mostly black boys who persecute him.

I was proud of my mom when she threw a neighbor out for saying *nigger*, but when black kids at school call me and others *honky* and *bitch*, I itch to retaliate. The bus stop nearest school, located in a tunnel under the Grand Concourse, is a dark and dank place where white kids endure insults, robbery and random punches. Rumor has it that two girls were raped by a black gang. No matter how cold it is, for self-protection we white kids have to drag ourselves to the next bus stop. Black friends can't stroll along unless they are dating one of us. Getting some off a white girl is considered the opposite of being a friend, so it meets militants' standards of acceptability.

Ralph's even tougher than I was. I learned early not to bring home complaints about kids and teachers. Until wising up that Mom's bravado was a raucous denial of powerlessness, I believed she would follow through on her threats to punch the teacher or punish the kid and his parents. Ralph's silence costs him more because his world is more dangerous than mine when I was young, and boys face substantial physical threats.

Sullen and angry, he is resigned to the fact that speaking up creates commotion, not change. Even though Mom doesn't drink anymore, her frenzied outbursts still terrify us more than punks. Her stability has been further undermined by exhaustion, apprehension and shame. She's tumbling downhill along with the Bronx.

I can't decide if my family is badly off because we are poor, or poor because we have been lazy, but Mom insists there's nothing wrong with us. "It's the system," she says; "Johnson can't deliver on the Great Society because we're all sinners." Her logic eludes me. Sometimes we're poor because of the system; sometimes we're deprived because we're depraved. She views the world through a dizzying kaleidoscope of competing worries about money, eternal punishment and the prospect of one of us being maimed or killed.

Mom doesn't notice the slower catastrophes that creep up on a person. She makes light of little Emma's afternoons gossiping with and about imaginary friends. "It's normal for a three-and-a-half-year-old. At least she's staying occupied." Alice receives attention only when she's sick. Mom pretends Ralph is a healthy, active boy who just happens to be beleaguered, but I've never even seen him run down the block. He has no friends and rarely speaks.

Praising Ralph as "a man of few words" strikes me as ridiculous, but I don't tell her so. She'll tell me I'm a girl of too many words and we'll be off and running. Some topics, however, shouldn't be dropped. Thinking she will relent because of the strap marks around Ralph's back and waist, for the third time in a month I offer to contact the Fresh Air Fund. Every once in a while I drop the Cranfords a card, thanking them for enriching my life, and I want Alice and Ralph also to experience a summer watching the stars and the moon instead of their backs.

"Ralph would be too hard for anyone to handle and Alice is too frail" is Mom's excuse for not letting them go.

"Maybe Ralph could be managed by a man and Alice would grow stronger in a place where she can run around outside more." I haven't even mentioned the fresh fruit and vegetables before Mom pounces.

"If the city doesn't shut down all the summer programs, they'll be perfectly fine staying home where they belong," she says, as if she doesn't remember being panicked about the Bronx a half hour ago. I suspect her inconsistency trains Ralph and Alice to prefer not to pay attention.

The idea of living through another hot summer in this apartment, skittish about the streets at night, tightens the small of my back into throbbing pain. I envision bonfires of garbage, children looting the supermarket and my mother screaming that her head is on fire, the way she does when she leaves the hair dye in too long.

Never one to step into the fray, Joan waits for Ralph to settle down in front of the TV and for Mom and me to stop sparring before sharing her news. This summer she'll be a paid counselor at a Bronx day camp that Alice and Ralph can attend for free. She and some of the other girls from the special program Joan is enrolled in have made a pact to protect each other's brothers and sisters from the rough kids.

After several years of tanking grades and attendance, in ninth grade Joan was scooped into a College-Bound program for underachievers. She and her friends see the same counselor weekly, and they support each other's efforts to absorb good advice as well as schoolwork. Now that she associates school with "cooperative social change," Joan cares about making an effort. "Many decent people of all types are trying to do something about the problems. We can be part of the solution." Her matter-of-fact manner reduces any sizzle of resistance.

Mom hugs Joan. "You're a good kid, you know that?" Then she turns to me, smiling. "You're all good kids."

22

MOTHER'S HELPER

No wonder many people in my neighborhood can't find jobs. Unless you scurry to the newspaper section soon after the library opens on Monday, you'll find only fragments of want ads butchered by razors. Buying two or three Sunday papers of your own adds up, but they're necessary. Then, if a job search extends outside New York, you have to pay for long-distance phone calls and travel for interviews. It takes money to make money.

I'm determined not to stay home this summer before eleventh grade and reconciled to my only option: working as a live-in mother's helper. Because my stacks of coins dwindle too quickly on wrong numbers and conversations that veer into wrong turns, I'll accept the first viable job I'm offered in Long Island or Westchester County.

After several botched and humiliating attempts, I develop my most cost-effective spiel. First, I identify myself and the ad. Second, to duck the suspicion leveled at the phoneless and to prompt immediate calls back, I briefly explain that I'm in a booth because Ma Bell has cut off services to my building in order to make extensive repairs. Third, I enthusiastically mention my large Irish-Catholic family. In a race against the meter, I can neither waste time on people's sly efforts to detect my color nor miss the opportunity to establish qualifications other than white skin. They listen for clues that you hail from a respectable family as much as evidence of baby-sitting experience.

Phone booths leave little room for the fancy footwork required of negotiations with potential employers. I feel self-conscious when I need to feel self-confident. Instead of politely observing from a distance, passersby gesticulate in imitation of my flailing movements as I take notes and count change in the narrow transparent cubicle with a kidney-shaped counter too small for balancing a notepad. People who want to make a call shrug their shoulders, mouth "Some Nerve" or give me the finger when they notice the sign I tape on the door: "Sorry, I will tie up the phone until noon."

Most of the women hiring mother's helpers fantasize about a teenage relative joining the family for a summer rather than a welfare kid from the Bronx whose parents can't drive her to Westchester or Long Island for a cup of coffee and a chat on the patio. They offer an allowance and a summerlong family reunion, whereas I'm seeking an interview and an income. It annoys me when these ladies claim working as a mother's helper for twenty dollars a week will cultivate disciplined work habits. I bet I've already held more jobs than they have.

I land a job taking care of eleven- and thirteen-year-old brothers, each one weighing more than I do. I'm only fourteen, but I bolster the lie that I am sixteen by underscoring the fact that

I'm headed for eleventh grade. At the interview, which I steeled myself for during the long ride on the Long Island Rail Road, my potential employer hinted that she expected "a little help" around the house—something she had not mentioned in the ad or on the phone. That's the formula for squeezing the most out of people, which is why I prefer hourly wage work. This woman had obviously rehearsed her argument that the wage included the cost of room and board in an elegant house. I countered that sleeping in the den and eating like a bird didn't add up to the cost of a housekeeper. My insistence that I would only watch the boys and clean up after myself probably helped make the case that I was mature enough to manage these hellions. Spirited, their mother calls them; rude, I think. It's a good thing it was late enough in the hiring season for this woman to accept my attitude.

I quickly master the routine so that Mrs. Woodmere, who asks me to call her Leila, won't regret hiring me. Each weekday morning I hound the boys through breakfast on time to dress and pack for a day at the beach club. My talent for duplicity serves me well in this job. As Leila and the boys sashay through the front door of the club, I shimmy and claw through a gap in a wire fence and then discreetly wend my way to their cabana. Because the Woodmeres refuse to pay the servant fee for a nonfamily member, at least I'm spared the fate of the black women who sweat in white uniforms all day. One of them, even though we are discouraged from mingling, slips me food from the kitchen after she sees me reading a library book collection of Gwendolyn Brooks poems, and we talk. "Shame on them!" she says when I explain I accepted the job without knowing I'd have to sneak into the beach club practically every day.

Once inside the club, I supervise the boys until day camp begins. Their mother rushes off to therapy, exercise, shopping or her sick mother's house. During the four blessed hours the boys are in camp, I lie on the beach browning my skin, reading, dreaming and awkwardly talking with some of the kids my age who hang out there. Wary about the poolside where most people congregate, I prefer the relative solitude of the waterfront. I can pass because I'm white, but too much friendliness could expose my true identity as an interloper and a servant. I'm used to lying to get a job, but this is the first time an employer has demanded daily deception from me.

When day camp ends, I hang out with the boys until their mother picks us up and I corral them while she makes dinner. I'm useless because I can't play or talk sports, but sometimes they soften and let me read the Hardy Boys to them. A couple of times they bash me with plastic bats, but I put a stop to that by shrieking that one of my friends in the Bronx who has a gun would come out on a moment's notice to teach them a lesson. The bogeymen of my childhood have become the handymen of my adolescence.

Live-in work turns out to be a different kind of hell from remaining home. It's not loud, but it's tense. Once I meet Mr. Woodmere, I understand the meanness and aggression of the boys. In the Bronx they'd be brandishing knives instead of slinging insults and an occasional plastic bat.

If not for the cost of the train, I'd escape to visit my family, Carol and Ann on my day off. Instead, I settle for the one free call a week I am allocated. Unaware that Joan and Mom stake out a phone booth at the prearranged weekly time, Mr. Woodmere is irritated that I'm adamant about calling home at eleven A.M. every Sunday regardless of his plans. He needles me about why my mother never calls: "Maybe she thinks you have nothing to say for yourself." It would never occur to him that some people can't afford three-dollar phone calls, even to their daughters.

One weekly dose of news from home suffices. When I'm home, I can help and I can detect exaggeration. On the phone, there's no time to sort out contradictions in the reports. Joan claims Ralph and Alice love camp; Mom insinuates Ralph rarely attends. To avoid inflaming their disagreements about tension in the neighborhood, I ask questions with the politeness of a stranger while aching to demand details about any signs that the skirmishes between residents and police in East Harlem are moving across the river to the Bronx. A Detroit-scale riot rumbles like approaching thunder in my imagination, but I bite my tongue.

From the window of the den one precious day when the boys are staying overnight with friends, I watch Mrs. Woodmere pull into the driveway after dropping them off and food shopping. She opens the car door and then slumps back down again, resting her head on the steering wheel in a pantomime of exhaustion I associate with older women. Rather than racing through page after page of Dickens to prove I can read a novel a week even when working full-time, I scamper out to help her unload the groceries. Her gratitude embarrasses me.

When I straggle into the kitchen a half hour later, she doesn't hear me because I am following house rules: no shoes inside! Her back toward me, she is leaning on the counter, head down. A tiny internal emotional motor vibrates her back and arms with sobs she muffles with her hands. This woman needs support from something more than a steering wheel and a counter.

I find my little voice, the one that has more sympathy than bravado. "Mrs. Woodmere, I'm sorry you're feeling so bad."

"I'll be fine in a second. Thank you." She pauses before turning around, and then faces me. "Is my mascara smeared?"

"I'll put away the groceries while you wash your face." I surprise myself by offering to pitch in on dinner.

She's either revived or well disguised, because she reminds me, without any rancor, that I negotiated only baby-sitting. This lady knows more about supervising people than her husband recognizes when he teases her for letting me get away with defining my job. On days when he blusters home from one of the four furniture stores he owns and manages, I withdraw. In contrast, her soft, sad tone and the spectacle of her scurrying to please her husband with a delicious dinner inspire me to yield a little, just as Dickens would have recommended. "When I take care of the kids eight hours, I shouldn't have to do anything else. But today I only spent six hours with them. So put me to work."

Easier said than done. Helping someone cook is as hard as dancing with a guy. Whether or not they can lead or you've practiced the move before, you're expected to follow gracefully. When you step on each other's toes and jerk in two directions at once, you can't tell if you're a clod or if your partner is a weak guide. I cook in tandem no better than I slow dance.

At first, Leila takes for granted that I know how to trim the steak, whisk fresh salad dressing, and fill the medium-size Wedgwood bowl with melon balls. I have to bug her for instructions. After she elaborates—she wants me to cut the fat off the sides of the sirloin using a serrated steak knife—I attack the slab of meat with what turns out to be a grapefruit knife. That's the one time she bleats in exasperation. No wonder she's tired. She's responsible for too many different types of knives, bowls and glasses.

After that child-free evening in the kitchen, Leila and I establish a new routine. I set the table and cut fruit every night. If Mr. Woodmere doesn't arrive on time for dinner, I assist in cleanup, partly by nagging the boys to scrape their dishes and pile them near the dishwasher for pre-rinsing. If he shows up, I stick with our previous agreement that I eat alone and clean up after myself only. There is no way I am scraping his plates.

Although Leila starts offering me the fish, steak and chicken she and her husband eat rather than the macaroni and cheese, frozen pizza and hot dogs the kids are permitted three days a week, she doesn't even hint that I should stick around and help when her husband is there. She's shielding her marriage from my spying.

Mr. Woodmere is twice the size of his wife. He intimidates her by booming questions about what she doesn't finish on a particular day before rambling about what he did and did not accomplish. When I hear them having sex one night, I ache for the mermaid suffocating under the weight of a beached whale.

All summer long I continue to read Dickens and Ayn Rand and write lengthy letters to my friends Carol and Ann. Ingesting thousands of words, I'm compelled to regurgitate paragraphs of descriptions, complaints and predictions about our upcoming Labor Day weekend sharing a room near the ocean, courtesy of Carol's new boyfriend, Larry. He's a master plumber she met at her first secretarial job in the High School Co-Op program that allows her to finish her degree while gaining supervised, paid work experience. Scrutinizing the photobooth picture she sent me of them smooching, I can see they've gotten close in only two months, but I'm confident Carol is levelheaded. She knows what she wants and exactly how far to go with a guy.

She's the one who declared we'd always be treated like trashy outsiders at the Catholic Youth Organization gatherings we had danced our way into in Pelham Bay, a middle-class section of the Bronx. Carol had been invited to a prom by someone who defied the expectation that he bring a Catholic high school girl, preferably one planning on college. He calculated that she was almost sanctified because she planned on junior college and only recently transferred to public school. One of his pals had been willing to court disapproval by taking me, but I blew him off. I didn't like him enough to spend a small fortune on professionally curled, starched hair and high heels to match a dress that resembles a frilly lamp shade. Ann and I preferred vicarious experience. We stationed ourselves behind a hedge to admire Carol's dignified limousine arrival on the Catholic college campus where many diocese high schools sponsor events. Then we hunched on her bed waiting for her to return home and recite every single detail. At two A.M., the apartment door slammed. Carol sobbed in Ann's arms: her date had insinuated that she owed him sex because dating her cost him the approval of his coach and priest.

After that, we stopped dressing up the CYO boys as knights in shining armor and looked to college boys. One night Carol wangled an invitation to a fraternity party at the Bronx campus of

New York University. As we lumbered through the dark, loud rooms, guys grabbed at us. Once the girl from school who brought us disappeared upstairs, we were introduced to people as "R.C. meat" and heard two guys promising each other sloppy seconds. Carol and Ann ended the evening vowing never to date college boys.

Carol's new boyfriend meets her standards. It takes discipline and skill to be a master plumber, he addresses her mom with respect and he's the marrying kind. She's sticking to Larry like Scotch Tape. Ann and I approve because he's willing to accept us as part of the package.

This guy is planning on setting me up with one of his friends as long as I don't act like a college girl, Carol writes. This way she and I can spend more time together than we've been able to since she started the Co-op regime. If I don't nail a scholarship for college, I can always pick up secretarial skills later, but I'm worried enough that this year I'll practice typing with her and Ann.

I cultivate a tan and attach great expectations to chocolate brown cotton Capri pants and a paisley halter top I buy specifically for Labor Day weekend. The outfit is my reward for this summer of self-consciousness and word-swallowing in the home of strangers. Mr. Woodmere thinks if you have the right car, furniture, house and neighborhood, you're licensed to criticize and bully people. At first I was disheartened when I heard him characterize me as "lacking in spontaneity," but then I was uplifted by umbrage. How's a girl going to be loose and authentic if she has to lie about her age and origins to snare a job that requires she steal like a cat burglar through a hole in a wire fence?

Throughout the summer Mr. Woodmere comments that despite my low-wattage personality, I am a good mother's helper, comparing me to their acquaintances who hired girls who get sick all the time or disappear for days with friends or family, or stay up so late they can't rise with the kids in the morning. These are the girls whose parents recommend earning extra cash, but they don't need it for the basics and expect to have fun over the summer.

One mother's helper across the street persistently lures me to goof off with her until she understands that I can't afford to get fired. Then, after I boast about having saved eighty dollars for clothes, she arranges for an ideal use of my day off. Her father drives me to his wholesale warehouse, where I spend hours selecting three cashmere sweaters, matching blouses and contrasting lined heather skirts which he hems on the spot. To repay her for the favor, I let her introduce me to pot, despite my qualms that she intends for us to get stoned every day until her babysitting summer ends.

Toward the end of the summer, with unusual urgency, Leila begs me to work Labor Day weekend because they want the kids out of their way when they throw their first big bash. Her mouth tightens and her tear ducts open when I insist on my plans. That night her husband threatens me with bad references if I depart before the final weekend of summer. He doesn't faze me one bit; I'm setting an example for Leila.

Soon I can't tell if she believes I deserve punishment or if she's registering remote-control commands from her husband. When I set the table while she slices, dices and stirs, she no longer talks to me. I'm still living here, but I miss her. Yet I'd rather hold my breath than apologize.

After boarding here all summer, a weekend in a rooming house with my friends sounds like paradise. My last two weeks with the Woodmeres are as tense as living with a toothache, fearing that the nerve will die. I wait for things to get worse, but I don't anticipate the nature of their revenge.

On my final day of work, when I politely ask for my bonus, since they have said nothing, Mr. Woodmere passes me five dollars "for a cab to the train station." Leila hovers in the background, head down. The boys, forbidden to hug me good-bye, cry. Determined to hide my tears, I depart in sullen silence. I was counting on thirty bucks to pay for the PSAT and an SAT tutorial that increases scores.

During the train ride home I compose a gushing, grateful letter to Miss Williams, the fairest boss of them all. Then, realizing I don't have the address in Mt. Vernon where she and Robert now live, I crumple and toss it.

From the train station I head straight to Carol's house so that she, Ann and I can travel to Rockaway together. As far as my family is concerned, I'm still in Long Island, but unable to call this Sunday. I figured if I told them I was heading to Rockaway for three days, Joan would want to tag along on her day off. I'm ready for older boys and fed up with younger kids.

No more baby-sitting, I vow. I lack the maternal instinct and the money stinks. These silent wars with employers in their houses leave me aching with as much self-consciousness as when I used to climb the stairs in school anxious to hide the holes in my socks and newspapers padding my shoes. In any case, kids deserve more than a begrudging caretaker. I begin to wonder if I'm jealous of loved children and phobic about any stirrings of warmth that could trick me into choosing motherhood one day, only to regret it the rest of my life. Something other than baby-sitting and Saturdays at Altman's will have to pay for PSATs, SATs and college applications.

Once I'm released from the Woodmeres' sphere, it occurs to me that they had to tolerate excessive moodiness from me. I now remember that the want ad clearly stated, "July 1 to Labor Day." Like prickly heat lodging in an unreachable section of my back, a suspicion creeps up on me that I am becoming like my mother and some community activists, half believing I deserve a special bonus for living at the bottom of the barrel. Mom has her reasons. Neither a full-time job nor welfare covers what she and the kids need. To get by, she breaks the law by working off the books for people who act like they're doing her a favor but pay less than minimum wage. Living in fear of getting caught for necessary lies while knowing she can't get ahead have made her bitter and furtive. As naturally as a child learns language, I've absorbed that bitterness and fear of being taken advantage of even though I make more than she does and have more chances. I stint on baby-sitting and even schoolwork to avoid the humiliation of getting caught believing anything other than the facts of life: disappointment is the most likely outcome of commitment and the poor stay poor while the rich get richer.

23

SERENDIPITY

Since our first visit to Rockaway Beach on Labor Day weekend, Ann and I have been welcomed by Carol's boyfriend Larry as if we are essential members of a queen's entourage. We know that he values us as an escort service in order to avoid having to trek to the Bronx to pick her up himself. Guys with mixed motives are preferable to those who are single-minded.

This third trip I'm starting to relax because I know what to expect. I recognize the stop before the dramatic moment when the train surges from underground onto the elevated tracks and briny, liquid air seeps through the doors. Carol, Ann and I confidently turn to the left when we leave the station, trusting that the cot, full-size bed and midget refrigerator at the boarding house will be clean even if the beds sag and the TV sounds like sandpaper rubbing gravel.

I care mostly about the timbre of the voice that greets me when we enter the bar where all of Larry's evenings begin. Tilting forward and lowering his voice, his brother John says, "Hey Mary," infusing those two syllables with paragraphs of affection. I think he's about to shake my hand, but instead he pulls me toward him by gripping my elbow. Then he shifts back into a regular voice as he says "Hey Ann." Now I realize the elbow is a transitional zone between the friendliness of a handshake and the intimacy of an arm around the shoulder.

Sequestered in a booth with me, John laughs without a hint of mockery at the unflattering picture on my obviously fake ID. In the company of Larry, I could have flashed a newspaper clipping and still been waved through by the bouncer. Twice John jumps up to introduce Ann to guys, impressing me by watching out for my chubby friend. He reminisces about twelfth grade. As far as he's concerned, Catholic high school was worth his parents' sacrifices because he learned discipline and the basic skills to score high enough on the police exam the second time. The more we drink, the more natural it is to drift from topic to topic, occasionally finding one we can sustain beyond a round of sentences.

I know John's all right when he says, "Oh yeah, I've had that one, too," after I describe dreaming of flying naked across a blue sky, scores of people admiring me or potential captors astonished by the form of my getaway. His version of the dream usually occurs over a baseball field and often involves catching a fly ball midair. We both briefly fall silent as the word naked floats through the space between us.

Despite our friendly glances, the other girls in the bar snub me and Ann. After washing my hands in silence in the bathroom, I shyly address one of them through her reflection in the mirror.

"I guess one mug of beer equals one trip to the bathroom."
She hesitates to speak until I've dried my hands and tossed the paper towel into the wastebasket while walking toward the door.

"This bar is too small to ignore people we see all night!" the girl admits, and then she explains her friends' behavior: two of them have had crushes on John for years and resent out-of-town girls stealing away the attention of a cute guy.

When I return to the booth, John glows in the dark, fluorescent with good looks, illuminated by his desirability to other girls. He tells me his father's a drunk and his mother a saint whom he thought about every day at sleep-away camp as a kid. The reciprocal, abbreviated family saga that I recite gives him an alibi to move closer to me. He slides from his side of the booth to mine and tips my face toward his: "You sure don't look black."

Sputtering about poverty and race, I'm revving up for an argument I can't steer through after splitting a pitcher of beer. Thank God he suggests a walk along the boardwalk. Alcohol, moonlight, a joint and late September evening chill at the ocean reduce the relevance of words. We seek sweaty communion, not verbal communication.

Two hours later we're back at the bar, where he lightly drapes his arms around my shoulder to steady both of us and to publicly post ownership. Shifty-eyed as a petty thief, I'm convinced that everyone knows I hungrily, drunkenly kissed him. When he walks me and Ann back to the boarding house, tightly clasping my hand, he warns her that he's keeping me all to himself after midnight Saturday. "If you can keep her up that late, she's yours," she says. Ann often teases me for crawling into bed by ten and rising by six.

Saturday night John and I begin by floating toward and receding from one another. We gaze fondly at each other through the noise and waves of back-slapping pals. He's about my father's height and exudes the same audacious aroma of cigarettes, beer and cologne.

John is irresistible, but I try to take note of his character when a friend ambles by to check me out and to rib him about becoming one of the men in blue. "If cops bashed more heads, niggers wouldn't trash so many blocks," this guy grouses, his theme being that cops cut too much slack to minorities moving into the neighborhood and to hippies undermining America.

John grins at his pal. "You've had your head bashed a couple of times, but your mother's driveway and lawn still look like a trash heap." Their rhythm of complaint, insult and familiarity suits me fine. I almost fit with these boys.

Since Labor Day weekend, I have submitted to the taboo about mentioning going to college. It threatens my friendship with Carol and Ann and makes these guys anxious that I might be smarter than them. I'm personally better off avoiding the topic anyway. At the slightest flicker of interest, I burst into flames of worries and jealousy. Other kids in the honors class don't have to work, as far as I know; they are able to study for the exams and have the time and money to learn about colleges and apply to several. Because they're not my friends, I can't discuss choosing and financing college with them any more than I can with kids who aren't going or with my family. I now sweep the issue into a soundproof room in my mind until the "college, college, college" chant that has motivated me for years has grown fainter. But I'm still nagged by concerns about finding work.

Being cool and casual about how you bring in money is required in most environments, including here at Rockaway Beach. Although the alcohol and the weight of carbonation in my belly usually allow me to act mellow, I can't help speaking up when one of John's friends boasts about all the chicks he meets as a messenger. "An hourly-wage job breezing around Manhattan sounds like freedom to me," I say. When a group of Rockaway wise guys volunteers that girls can't be messengers, I protest. "There's no reason girls can't do the work. We can do things besides wait on guys in offices and houses."

Carol yanks me into the bathroom, nervous that my speechifying courts Larry's disapproval. But outside, John teases me. "You're as much of a firecracker as a redhead." He rolls his eyes slightly when I repeat my vow to nail an outdoor job, but then takes my side. "You know, one of the reasons I'm going to be a cop is to avoid sitting behind a desk." He talks slowly, as if afraid of making a mistake, just as I talk fast, to keep people from challenging my mistakes.

Like his brother, John prefers a date who dips in and out of his vicinity so that he can ride a bar stool with his friends while having something to look forward to after midnight. Thus liberated, Carol, Ann and I angle our way into the middle of the dance floor. Legs vibrating, heads bobbing, fingers snapping, we're oiled with a light sweat that warms our world. Our bodies insist on being in motion; dance is for us what sport is to boys.

If I graze too long in John's company, a swarm of bees buzzes in my brain. *We should be talking. He should be drinking less. I should be in bed.* Returning from the dance floor to John's sphere, I am drawn out of myself toward him, as if all along he has been my invisible partner. Thanks to Ballantine, pot, saltwater, and the Righteous Brothers, I experience him as an enchanted adjacency rather than the attentive interlocutor for whom I thought I yearned. After dropping off Ann on Saturday night, we kiss, mumble and fumble for hours in his car. Sonic signals and chemical destiny draw us closer. In this sodden darkness, I can project onto him any image that pleases me.

We are boyfriend and girlfriend by Sunday, the same day I spot an ad in the paper for an afternoon messenger at a carpet company. Before hearing John's friend quacking about tits and tips, I probably would have ignored an ad for a guy's job. But years of exploring the Bronx on my own have built my confidence that I can roam without getting lost or kidnapped.

I easily persuade the carpet retailer in midtown Manhattan to hire me, once he overcomes his amusement at a girl applying. His primary questions are: Can you read a subway map? Walk two hours a day, rain or shine? Start immediately? Two days later we are employer and employee.

Just as there's a diamond district and two streets in midtown Manhattan dotted with stores that sell musical instruments, there's a buzzing carpet industry around Park Avenue in the 20s and 30s. Although occasionally I'm sent to private homes to pinch-hit for one of the three salesmen, mostly I fetch and return samples to showrooms and factories. With receptionists, I practice my Altman's persona; with freight elevator operators, my Spanish. A sack slung over my right shoulder and instructions in my pea-coat pocket, I swagger as if I'm hauling pirate's booty. Mapping my route with flare, some days I finish early. Instead of docking me for efficiency, the carpet store owner and the woman who is his executive assistant pay me for three hours even if I only work two.

John is impressed that I went after the job, but hints I shouldn't taunt his friends with proof that girls can be messengers or bore them by talking about details. I accept his terms. Being a girlfriend resembles being an employee. You're required to follow rules and cues about topics of conversation, chains of command and break time.

I remind myself that I am lucky after all: on one magical weekend I stumbled simultaneously upon a perfect boyfriend and an ideal job. I may refuse to count my blessings, but I cherish coincidence and serendipity.

24

ED SULLIVAN

After incessant worry about landing a job, I've ended up with two. Not only am I making minimum wage as a messenger, but B. Altman's wrote to me about part-time openings before the Christmas rush. Two nights a week and all day Saturday I now assist the commissioned sales staff in Better Blouses. We sell ugly blouses swirling with colors and designer's signatures, some of them for more than forty dollars. Fortunately, we also sell beautiful, thick cotton blouses through which only X-ray eyes could detect a sliver of bra strap or lacy slip. It costs more to dress with fashionable modesty.

Some customers stare quizzically, expecting older saleswomen, and then relent as soon as I speak. There's no trace of the Bronx in this girl's crisp, perky accent. I strain my throat and psychic muscles in my eagerness to please. After hanging on a customer's every word as if I'm listening to the host of a game show who could funnel me millions of dollars and a passport to exotic locales, I speak with deliberate caution, braking on my natural tendency to talk long and fast. "We do indeed have cotton blouses with covered buttons, including some pale blue and sparkling white ones recently arrived from Paris."

In this world, being prim is allowed if you are competent, whereas on the streets near home or the bars in Rockaway it makes you a target for those anointed to punish the vulnerable and the stuck up. According to my crude social calculus, the best people are those who speak clearly, finish their sentences, curse selectively and say "It's time to sit down to dinner" rather than "You'd better feed your face before there's nothing left on the table." Work is about metamorphosis as much as money.

A buyer in Better Dresses praises my vocabulary and steers me to gorgeous, affordable clothing. At first I don't realize that she is tucking away size 8 sale items and then retrieving them when it's time for final clearance reductions. "Don't worry, we won't get in trouble," she assures me. "Management doesn't care as long as the items are end of season." It turns out that this is how many of the unmarried saleswomen dress well enough to work in upscale stores.

Faux pearl and satin buttons, jacquard, eyelet and Egyptian cotton enter my life. I stroke them like pets. Fabrics absorb my sensual energy almost as much as John.

The buyer also offers me tips on makeup, hair care and perfume that will disguise my smoky odor. I flatly deny smelling like an ashtray. How could I? I only occasionally puff and I'm out and about more than I'm home or in the bars where cigarettes taint the air. Her interest in cultivating me collapses when I fiercely insist that I won't use cosmetics or fuss with my hair.

Now that I have a boyfriend, I admire my five-six, ninety-nine-pound frame. But I check my face in a mirror only for dirt, swiftly averting my eyes from the looming specter: yellow buck teeth, stringy hair, pointy nose and eyes hollowed by sadness. Posed two feet from a full-length mirror, I happily grin at a headless mannequin, a clotheshorse. I am a contented torso that disowns its own face and mane.

The two times I experimented with lipstick, my teeth looked like canvas spotted with red. Since then I have recoiled from the spectacle of women whipping out compacts to admire themselves spreading and tightening their lips to apply greasy color. Why would they do such a thing in public? Mascara was a different story. After only four days of fluttering, darkening and curling my eyelashes, I realized my untreated eyes looked shrunken and dull in contrast. I didn't want to become addicted to lush lashes and compelled to check myself in mirrors several times a day. Lucky for me, more and more women are ditching their cosmetics bags. Thin is in, and unadorned, long straight hair at last admired.

I can spend most of my income on clothes because I don't have to worry about where my next meal is coming from anymore. A month ago Carol began showing up at school with an extra sandwich packed by her mother. Mrs. Dyer doesn't earn much as a secretary, but she assured me she could spare a few extra pieces of bread and cold cuts for me to wolf down during my train ride to Manhattan right after the school day ended at noon. Each day I looked forward to what I'd find within the crisp folds of the reused wax paper.

The sandwiches become unnecessary by December. Carol and

Larry now sneak me into the Metropolitan Life cafeteria, where employee benefits include a balanced meal. Instead of eating a sandwich as the train to Manhattan plunges ahead, I speed read; when it stops, I scribble. My history and English papers write themselves, and I don't reread them. Schoolwork has become another chore to get through on my way to something else. Academic goals are merely a familiar shape momentarily flashing in the opposite direction on a subway train. I'm not sure if I'm glimpsing an apparition or substantial possibility. Once at the resplendent cafeteria, I gobble my entrée and two sides like an athlete in training. Then I sprint to the carpet company.

Filching free lunch from a company is easier than freeloading off Mrs. Dyer, but she insists on continuing to supply me with sandwiches for snacking. She worries that I am too skinny and need more energy for running around Manhattan. Carol's mother knows more about how I spend my time than my own mother does.

I want to be like my sister Lacey, out of the house by sixteen, but to do it by going to college. Then I will have my pick of executive secretary jobs. I like the sound of *executive* more than the sound of *saleslady* or *waitress* or *mom*. Because Mrs. Dyer held a job even when Carol was a baby, she encourages what she calls my work ethic.

I don't envy the kids I see hanging out on the streets near home. They're always waiting for their father or one of their grown brothers to take them for rides and dreaming of the day when they'll own cars. They seem besieged by boredom, deprived of a vision of the monumental stone buildings with murals, like Met Life, to which they could be whisked by public transportation.

185

Still, I long to spend a Saturday reading for pleasure, watching TV and turning a rope for hours so that Joan and Alice can jump. These days I'm as available to my family as a devoted, divorced father who visits for birthdays, holidays and such special events as weddings and accidents. When I'm around, I do what I can when I notice a problem. I rush to the rescue if Joan's unable to go to school because she has no money for sanitary napkins or Alice is disappointed because Mom can't come up with two dollars for a class trip. Swearing him to silence, I slip Ralph lunch money, knowing he'd rather starve than walk the gauntlet of the cafeteria food line at school where the workers gape at the sight of big kids slapping younger kids and walking off, laughing, with their plates.

My generosity is furtive. I dread my mom becoming dependent on my contribution and making even less of an effort to bring in extra cash. She's bone tired and too old to land a shift working tables in Manhattan. But if she keeps coming up with excuses, the owners of the two coffee shops in our vicinity will stop offering her occasional hours off the books. Her working days will be over. I don't want to think of my mother as one of those people who treats welfare like a hammock instead of a safety net.

Mom has her eyes on the fruits of my labor, while I hone my stinginess. When she hints that I should help out more, I parse my words like a businessman who might shop at B. Altman's. "Welfare pays for my share of the rent; I ask you for nothing else."

"Okay, have it your way," Mom sullenly replies. Now home feels a lot like the Woodmeres', only more crowded. Mom doesn't yell at me anymore; most of the time she treats me like a boarder who should be shunned for not paying but for some reason can't be evicted. I get up early and come home late four or five nights a week.

Being an employee in Manhattan spawns more surprises than being a daughter, a sister, a neighborhood girl or a student. One day when Carol, Ann and I parade down Fifth Avenue, a vaguely familiar man approaches us, with a big smile. In my neighborhood I would never smile back at someone I wasn't sure I could identify by name; he might be a pervert. But I'm flanked by friends in midtown Manhattan, where we can safely beam back at him until he stops right in front of us, putting out his hand. It's Ed Sullivan, the long-faced host of the Sunday-night variety show. He praises the exact things that would elicit mockery in my neighborhood. He compliments us on our appearance, contrasting us to sloppy hippie girls, and grills us about where we live and go to school. Then he ceremoniously passes us a card with a phone number, encouraging us to call whenever we want free tickets to orchestra seats for one of his shows. "The camera appreciates pretty girls to scan," he says, and floats away, like an angel.

Wearing coordinated, quality clothing is the toll we willingly pay to stride along wide avenues, our eyes traveling from shop windows to ornate buildings. Caught in a rainstorm, we can duck into a store without being regarded as thieves and interlopers. Instead of hacking my way through a thicket of needy children and threatening punks near home, in Manhattan I saunter in a clearing from which I can see the horizon. Who knew that cardigans and knee-length tent dresses could also spirit open the door to free, center orchestra seats? The ushers at the Ed Sullivan show scurry to make us comfortable. As soon as the "Quiet" sign blinks, we hush in unison. Mom flatters me by watching every night we attend and, in the voice of Topo Gigio, the Italian puppet, reports on how beautiful we look the few times the camera catches us.

Because I am a member of an audience, not a crowd, my senses come alive. For the first time in my life, I listen to music by separating the sounds of different instruments and letting them merge together again. When the lights dim, my friends and I glimpse, as if in candlelight, each other's pleasure at seeing the Lennon Sisters and the Lovin' Spoonful in person. Before each show we scarf down half-price banana splits at the coffee shop next to the studio, courtesy of the Sullivan show. We are debutantes facing a world that is eager to welcome us as long as we're punctual and properly dressed, even if we do have to wipe the smiles off our faces before the train deposits us back home in the Bronx.

25

ADVICE

When the guidance counselor notices me wearing a guy's ring, she pulls me aside in the hall. "You are going to college, you hear me?" she barks. "What are you doing going steady with a guy six years older than you, a cop no less?" Another cop-hater, I think. I had no idea Mrs. Brustein even knew who I was and wonder how she found out about John. At least I'll be able to talk to someone about college.

When I finally nail an appointment with her one Friday, she tells me I look more cheerful than she has ever seen me and she sure hopes it's not that boyfriend making me happy. I catch her drift and change the subject. "I landed a great job. I can save the money to apply to colleges next year."

She's not interested in hearing about carpet samples; nonetheless I sense that she is sincerely watching out for me even though she was disappointed by my PSAT scores. "What makes smart girls like you come out just above average on this test, huh? You should have done better."

I don't tell her I was hung over the day of the exam, of course; I'm not even sure that's why I felt blank and tired. Taking the exam too seriously would have betrayed my friends. Maybe I was poisoned by doubt that making an effort would be worth it. Before I can answer her question, she says that I should stop worrying about paying for applications; some schools waive fees for kids like me.

"Why didn't someone tell me that sooner?" I ask, with no expectation of reply.

After scanning a form I completed for her records, she challenges my preference for Catholic colleges. "You're restricting yourself too much."

"I want to go to a quiet place where kids don't protest." I don't mention that by some accident of affiliation all my close friends except Paula have been Catholic and I avoid kids who do a double take when I say there are seven children in my family.

Raising her voice as if preparing to cough and speak at the same time, she tries to straighten me out; "College students are fighting for important social change."

Words like *fighting* and *protesting* blur in my mind into a single, continuous-playing newsreel of unkempt people overturning automobiles, making vulgar gestures and disturbing my peace. I can't offer her more explanation than "I'm trying to get away from places where people riot." If I keep talking, my voice will run away from me into a shout. Once I'm sucked into orbits of disagreement, I can get as loud as a washing machine agitator with a broken fin.

Our views are incompatible and I shoot down her suggestions as if they are enemies of my future. Radcliffe College has special programs for disadvantaged girls like me, but I'm not putting my future in hock by borrowing one to three thousand dollars a year. Looking at my record to avoid making eye contact with me, she says I could probably go to Columbia for free tuition if I lived at home; I'd rather join a carnival.

We speak past each other, and soon she's looking at her watch instead of my file. She points a finger at me: "You're worrying about the wrong details and wasting this appointment. Read some of the catalogs and articles in the outer office and come back when you've thought through what you want." She shoves seven fat catalogs at me after I solemnly swear I'll return them on Monday.

Her time is commandeered by the kids whose parents leave the phone messages that are pierced to a thin stake on her desk. My attention is scattered to the winds of divided loyalties. Talking with most people makes me anxious; only walking between sites to collect and distribute squares of carpet frees my mind to daydream and think thoughts that transcend routine. Most of the time I'm focused on keeping up with my schedule: Monday through Friday afternoons at the carpet company, Wednesday and Friday evenings and all day Saturday at Altman's, late Friday and all of Saturday night with John, and Sunday for homework and Ed Sullivan when he's recording.

At first when Mom announces we're all heading to Lacey's apartment for an early dinner on Sunday, I beg off, daunted by how much time it will take to read catalogs that total over a thousand pages all together. But when I begin flipping through them Sunday morning, I realize they are mostly course listings, page after page of small print paragraphs it doesn't make sense to digest now. I pause to study the pages on financial aid and to look at pictures, all the while distracted by warm, visceral recollections of Saturday night with John and by Joan's raspy snore as she lies beside me in a deep sleep.

What I discover makes me want to crawl back under the covers: in college you have to share a room with one or two other people, unless you pay extra. I could end up living with night owls, or snobs, or girls who wake up talking. It never occurred to me that in a dorm room I might have to maintain office and shop floor demeanor instead of savoring the solitude I crave. Quickly, I arrive at a preference for a school that either has no triples or allows students to live off campus no later than sophomore year.

For years I have imagined my own narrow room, spare and serious as a monk's, where no one can intrude without knocking. Solitude is part of the appeal of the College of Mount Saint Vincent, a tiny colony of churchy buildings in Riverdale which I walked to and from at the cost of the soles of a pair of shoes. The sight of quiet girls behind glass panes on the second floor of the library reminded me of a class trip to the Metropolitan Museum of Art, where I was drawn to a room of Dutch paintings of women framed by mirrors and windows.

I can't expect such stillness at state universities where students have to bunk with strangers in clusters of buildings resembling projects. Everyone smiles in the catalog photos of a crowded cafeteria and of a circle of students gathered in the common rooms in a new complex of an upstate SUNY campus that Mrs. Brustein wanted me to read about. But I see chaos. No wonder private schools cost thousands more than public.

In only one hour I've decided I'm not applying to any of the seven schools Mrs. Brustein wanted me to consider. I can't even remember which ones she called *reach* schools and which ones *safe*. The College of Mount Saint Vincent looms large in my mind even more than it did after I visited. It's going to be number one on my list. I'm choosing college like a blindfolded child reaching into a fishbowl to pick one name out of three hundred.

Surprisingly free for the day because the catalogs monopolized only one hour and Sullivan isn't recording tonight, I please my family and myself. "Hey Mom, I've finished sooner than expected; I can go to Lacey's."

"How good of you," she teases me. "Lacey would have been disappointed if you didn't show."

I bump hips with her. "Me, too. We haven't been on a journey in a while."

Although I can't bring myself to say it, I want to tell my mom what occurred to me the other day. One of the freight elevator operators at Karastan Carpet asked how a skinny girl like me could be a messenger. Without skipping a beat, I replied, "My mom always encouraged us to be walkers." The rest of the shift I was accompanied by memories of the days before food stamps, when Mom used to corral all of us for the journey to the outposts where we collected free bags of rice, tins of beef, cans of peanut butter, long blocks of cheddar cheese and boxes of powdered milk. As toddlers, Ralph and Alice were ordered to remain cooped up in carriages all the way to our destination, usually a church basement, abandoned army arsenal, or hospital. Once there, they weren't allowed to romp even when we waited on line for hours. "You want food, you stay still," Mom said.

They had to reserve their strength for the long walk home, when the carriages would be stocked with goods. You only have to learn once that a shopping cart isn't strong enough to carry the heavy items. Marching and skipping back with the kids, pushing the carriages for what felt like miles, Jackie, Joan and I relished Mom's praise that we were all growing into strong walkers. She even let us lead people on when they approached the carriages, wanting to see the babies that added to our large promenading family. Smiling and friendly, we lifted the blankets to expose the precious cargo of food we cherished as much as any infant.

These days in New York we wouldn't dare to tease strangers. Crime and potential riots threaten all five boroughs. Accepting Lacey's invitation to view her new apartment in Queens has taken on the dimensions of a complicated foreign journey. The first time we tried to go, there was a transit strike. Then came rioting in East New York. One thing after another got in the way, but we're finally able to pay our collective tribute to Lacey's hard-working, drug-free life.

"I've come a long way," Lacey muses, as she leads a tour through the two-bedroom high-rise apartment she shares with Dana. Then she opens the drapes to display the skyline of Manhattan in the distance.

After making another circuit through the living room and kitchen, Mom looks mournful. "What I could do with a place like this."

Dead silence is followed by Lacey exploding. "Don't try and make me feel guilty. I work hard for what I get, and I've given you plenty." Dana, who has been slumped in a corner chair, rises to glare at Mom.

I knew Lacey would not be able to maintain the gracious hostess act for long. Her long, painted nails and perfect beehive hairdo mean that she's the femme in her relationship, but not a pushover in the family. She's in costume, just like all her fabulous friends in the photos framed and displayed throughout the apartment.

Men who dress up like women have to work much harder than femmes to pull it off. Dana has it the easiest. She wears the same kind of gray or beige chinos and flannel shirts all the time. Alberto VO5 keeps her hair in place all day. Her personality seems to stay in the same place all the time, too. Lacey is proud that her stone-cold butch is so handsome, but I can tell by the way she flutters that she wishes Dana talked more or would help out. Dana simply sits there, except when she hugs Lacey in support for the spat with Mom, and then she sits down again.

Mom is sulking, Ralph is skulking until it occurs to him to capture attention by peeing in the kitty litter, and Alice is wordlessly studying the fragmented reflections of her face in a large crystal bowl. Emma and Joan stick to Mom like bodyguards. The visit is not going well.

Finally Lacey makes the first gesture toward peace by bringing up one of Mom's favorite topics: "What d'ya think about Lindsay these days?"

Dana huffs, "Paying tribute to Caesar," and then settles back into silence.

Before I know it, they are happily chewing on Mayor Lindsay, the only Republican Mom ever voted for. "He'd better deliver," she threatens. "New York is going to hell in a handbasket. He's as handsome and smart as JFK was, but New York ain't no Camelot." Mom worries Lindsay doesn't have enough backbone to send out the cops if there are riots this summer. Understanding the causes of disorder shouldn't lead to tolerating it, she declares. She's afraid the city government is licensing looting by handing excuses to thugs, going along with the idea that poverty causes violence. As far as I'm concerned, opportunistic black militants are pumping up gangs with political justifications for violence. I'm a natural at defensive, wayward antagonism, so I recognize it when I see it.

Joan and I perk up at the idea of disasters that are bigger than the family. Thinking about New York is like watching a horror movie or a science-fiction film. We're waiting for the earth to cave in and planning on joining an advanced tribe of people forced to live in underground caves or catacombs. Joan suggests that boys in our neighborhood, where no one we know has pocketed a college deferment from Vietnam, could join us there if they promise to behave.

Alice is satisfied just having her own spoon, something she has wanted for as long as I can remember. She resents the fact that when we have tea at home we share one spoon and Joan torments her by licking it before passing it on. Because Lacey owns a dishwasher, she'll let us use as many plates and spoons as we need. I'm eating in a magazine spread where it might be acceptable to use my knife and fork European style, as long as I don't call any particular attention to myself. It wouldn't be right to steal the scene away from Lacey, who is working hard to live in the kind of place Mom can only long for.

In record time Lacey moved up from wrapping packages and

working the cash register to being an accounts payable clerk at Woolworth's. When she learned she wouldn't be promoted to supervisor without a junior college degree or ten years of experience, she began filling out job applications elsewhere, granting herself something called an associate's degree even though she doesn't even have a high school diploma. Now she's making enough money to save for a brand-new car.

Lacey and Mom are happy again and carrying all of us along with them, so I try not to worry about Lacey ending up in jail for fraud. I'm learning that sometimes you have to lie and steal just a little to get what you deserve; I draw the line at violence and looting.

After we finish dinner and return to the couch, Mom turns to Ralph and Alice to play one of their favorite games. Paying attention to her pantomime, they have to complete whatever sentence she begins.

She says, "I'm expecting . . ." and then starts waving her hands around and whishing and whooshing. Alice says "a tornado" and Ralph says "a hurricane." She helps them pronounce "apocalypse."

When Mom's gestures calm down and her smile widens, Joan says "windfall," probably thinking of some combination of the meal we have just eaten and a mild hurricane. Ralph hugs a pillow against his chest and Alice yells, "Baby."

"God forbid," Mom says, "but it would be a miracle for someone my age."

Lacey shakes her head at me to stifle my birth-control speech, which she thinks no fifteen-year-old should make. There was a *Daily News* editorial against making the pill available to teenage girls, as if it's the pill that causes sex. Maybe someone should write an editorial banning horny, aggressive boys from access to girls. It seems clear that if teenage girls are stupid enough to go all the way, adults should be smart enough to give them the pill.

We all know that if Jackie had used it, she wouldn't be marrying Martin next month, racing against time, hoping her belly won't show. He is the first one Jackie got serious about after Bad News went the way of the dinosaurs. At least Martin is not the type to mess up a girl's face.

After dinner Mom and Lacey talk about the wedding as if it's a good thing. Excited about being flower girls, especially once Lacey promises to fix their hair, Alice and Emma practice walking down the aisle of the apartment, waving at each door as if secret guests are about to emerge, smiling and full of compliments.

Then Lacey, taking advantage of the restored peace, proposes that Dana, after all the only man in the family, give Jackie away. Mom looks trapped: "It's up to Jackie."

"Jackie has already agreed," Dana bellows.

"So be it," Mom mutters, resigned and defeated, until she revives. Changing her voice to a high pitch and crooking her right arm at the elbow to show off a limp wrist, she squeals, "This will make it a special wedding."

People like Lacey and Dana are called queers and are also called special. I love it when antonyms become synonyms.

At the wedding, Dana doesn't come across as special at all. She's just a regular guy in a tuxedo as far as anyone can tell, although the priest nixed the idea of her giving Jackie away. To compensate, Mom introduces Dana to Martin's relatives as Lacey's husband, winking at Lacey when she says, "I hope Jackie and Martin will be as happy as these two."

I hear Dana whispering to my mother, "Sandy, you are a remarkable woman. Lacey and I tell everyone how accepting you are." Dana's not even lowering her voice to sound more like a man. She means what she's saying, and she's probably right.

Jackie looks gorgeous, girlish and deliriously happy as a bride. In their little pink dresses, paid for by Lacey, Emma and Alice float around the reception hall, carried by their crinolines. They distribute flowers to the guests, glowing at all the attention. Emma and Alice have big personalities, just like Jackie. Emma zeroes in on men. Alice loudly chats and laughs with everybody, but doesn't listen much. Joan, Ralph and I hold back, contented and shy, waiting for the cake to be cut.

After all these years of wishing Jackie away, it's weird to think she's moving out forever and going to make me an aunt. Unable to contain a growing sense of panic, I plead with Joan to promise not to have a baby until she's at least twenty-one. Her response makes me happy. "I'm not having a baby until after I finish college," she says with confidence.

It turns out that she had perked up at a news feature on Lyndon Johnson stumping for financial aid for poor kids to go to college. LBJ was talking directly to Joan about her future, just as a priest at a lectern sometimes seems to directly address everyone in the church as an individual soul. "Be good and your afterlife will be better than this one." I'm not going to burst her balloon by

199

sharing what I've learned about the lack of privacy in college. What matters the most is that she and I can leave home by going to college instead of walking off on the arms of men who are drunk as skunks and can't afford honeymoons.

26

RUMORS OF RIOTS

"It's as though we don't even exist," Mom moans, and then she begins to cry, folding forward around her stomach, her whole body rumpled.

Joan and I cry, too.

We didn't take the events of the past two days as a sign of our doom until watching the local news tonight. Officials are claiming that, unlike Chicago, D.C. and Baltimore, New York did not experience rioting as a result of the assassination of Martin Luther King, Jr. New York has experienced only what they call "negligible pockets of disorder."

"Tell that to the store owners who won't be able to get insurance again, you stupid, lying bastard," Mom screams.

Maybe we've always known that our community's grief and fear are negligible to the powers that be. A pall spreads over the room: a proponent of peace died violently and is now being violently mourned.

First there were the rocks, firecrackers and cherry bombs. After the third object crashed through our kitchen window and set some of the clothing drying overhead on fire, we knew it wasn't random. We were being targeted. We turned off all the lights and waited out the night, praying we'd learn King had not been killed by a white policeman, wishing, deeply wishing he had not been killed at all.

"But who would believe us?" we wondered. Our only solution was self-imprisonment. It's a good thing we finally had a telephone.

Then there were the notes under the door in the morning. DEATH TO WHITEY. WHITEY BETTER MOVE ON. Someone in our building must want our apartment for a relative, and we knew none of our black and Puerto Rican friends in the building would dare to do anything to help us by saying we're not the Man. They live in fear, too.

It's true that we have a few more options because we're white. If landlords see Mom and one or two of us, maybe we can escape to a block that is still populated by some white people and employed minorities. But Mom gets bleary-eyed and feels exhausted contemplating another move without the help of movers, and they are out of the question. I've stopped telling any of the black and Puerto Rican kids in my building about my jobs, because they'd never get hired. You have to talk white to be in sales. White skin, it seems, opened doors I thought I had elbowed my way through solely with gumption and random luck.

But our advantages are miniscule, Mom says, and fast disappearing. "There's no way any of you can get one of those nice summer jobs through the youth program; all the plums are being given to minorities. They're making up for lost time and we're gonna be the losers. So be it."

Then Alice, stir crazy, snuck out of the house, not believing we were in a war zone. She was thrown up against the wall by a gang of black boys, and just as quickly released. They slouched off after a lady in the building blasted them about how it would break their mothers' hearts if they knew about such good boys flipping into bad. She marched Alice upstairs and told Mom, "Nobody should be out on the streets for the next couple of days, especially people like you. God bless!"

All over the city, people are mugged, store windows smashed by looters and children beaten by other children. Everybody has a different story about what the cops are up to. The two cops in our precinct say their hands are tied. They are not supposed to react when people hurl bottles and names at them. The disrespect is getting to them. It's a good thing their fathers aren't on the force anymore. The old guys would never have put up with the coddling of criminals and made hard-working people live in fear.

They must forget we're on welfare, too; they think it's just black and Puerto Rican people who can't or don't want to work. But they usually catch themselves and say, "Not everybody, not everybody. There are a lot of hard-working Negroes who want us to crack down."

What we hear from neighbors and on the news is entirely different: "Cops are the instigators; they swing billy clubs at mothers and kids whenever they get the chance."

"The language cops use can't be repeated in front of kids."

"Ever see a cop pay for his own meal?"

"Drugs are all over the place because the cops are on the take."

"They'd act different if the dealing was going on in their neighborhoods."

I don't want to believe the police are part of the problem; they've always been nice to us, apologizing that they can't do anything about the guy who stands in his window exposing himself or the candy-store owner who strokes little girls. I tell anyone who will listen that my boyfriend, John, wants to be a cop so that he can do good.

Just when we're getting over what we call the MLK riots, the Columbia kids start rioting and there's talk of insurrection in Harlem. We keep hearing about Up Against the Wall Motherfucker and not a thing about Vietnam. Barnard girls call cops pigs and dare them to eat the bloody tampons they fling at them. Off camera the cops call them "crazy kike bitches."

Mom dreams of her number coming in so that she and the kids can escape the city and live someplace peaceful. After hours of such talk drifting through the house like a narcotic, she admits, "That's not gonna happen," and devises an alternative plan. "We'll never find an apartment this big, but we can get a place where the hallway doesn't feel like a gauntlet. Mary will jump ship soon, so we'll settle for a two-bedroom farther uptown." She says she knows better now. Only a fool takes an apartment near a park and a schoolyard.

Mom has a point. Any place that attracts crowds will include the bad element that ruins it for everyone else. But I wish she wouldn't keep berating me because I'm going away to college and abandoning the family.

I can't show how scared I am about being on my own, or it will discourage the kids. Joan has to believe that college is normal, not a betrayal of the family that leaves you floating in dangerous waters all alone. I want Alice and Emma to know that going to school leads to something other than Mom's rejection and classroom brawls. And Ralph, poor Ralph, needs to see that most encounters with the outside world do not leave bloodstains. When Bobby Kennedy is killed, Ralph glares at the TV like a zombie and nods like a robot at Mom testifying that this is the final sign that an apocalypse will arrive during the summer of 1968.

Yet the summer flies by for me and for them, as far I can tell. The worst that happens at home is scraped knees and Ralph spraining his wrist practicing gymnastics at camp. I work full time and devote the remainder of my time to John. By his side, I'm learning to hold my liquor but not my tongue. Weekend after weekend, in the bars that set the parameters for our social lives, I prove I cannot be trusted. I need a muzzle more than lipstick. Carol and Ann voluntarily serve as my censors. "Stop being sarcastic about the war; have a little respect for the number of people here who've lost brothers." "Why do you have to tell people your oldest sister is a lesbian?" "Lighten up, they'd never tell those jokes if there was a Jew in the bar."

John doesn't care about what I say to him as long as I don't irritate his friends. Alone, my monologues help us pass the time. We understand our roles. I'm entertainment; he's audience. I'm the high school girl; he's the rookie cop. We are both primed for recreational coupling rather than dialogue, but he respects my limits as if I'm the Virgin Mary.

My namesake has haunted me as long as I can remember. At

first glance, she represents purity. The Immaculate Conception sounds hygienic, as if you can scrub yourself free of sexuality and painlessly produce perfect babies, without breaking water or bleeding. But by high school I considered the Virgin Mary a celebration of a destructive lie. If you are raised to believe that you can get pregnant without sex, you can be tricked just as easily into thinking the reverse, that you can do it without paying the consequences. No matter what, you're expected to value virginity as an unqualified good. So for years I have preserved my mythical virginity. Technically I lost it when I was thirteen. Bleeding heavily for a ninth day, I couldn't leave the house without appearing bow-legged from wearing two sanitary napkins. Finally, I was frightened enough to beg my mom to take me to the emergency room. Before I knew it, she had signed some papers and I was a specimen assigned to gynecology interns who pounced on opportunities to examine young vaginas. Legs in stirrups and privates propped open, covered with a white sheet, I read comics and occasionally acknowledged an introduction to yet another medical student who was there to take a look and poke around, as if I was a cave, with neither nerve endings nor modesty. By the time a nurse came in to clean up, shocked to find me in that position for more than an hour, one of my legs was asleep and I was tormented by the conviction that only a serious illness could explain the large number of examiners. She was the one to deliver the diagnosis: I was a perfectly healthy, heavy bleeder, but should watch out for anemia.

Technically, I lost my virginity to a gaggle of interns and my innocence about the nobility of teaching hospitals on the same day. All the way home, Mom assured me I was still a virgin, as if that was bothering me. She felt bad enough without me moaning about the anemia of resources that means you have to expose yourself to hordes of men to receive medical care.

27

SCHOOL STRIKES

Joan has been chewing her nails for two days. Teachers are striking, yet again. Word in the neighborhood is that this third strike proves that the Jewish teachers don't give a shit about black and Puerto Rican kids and that the Bronx, too, should seize control of its own schools rather than letting Brooklyn fight the teachers' union alone. The negotiation between the union and people fighting for community control has turned into a vicious battle between Jews and blacks in the Ocean Hill–Brownsville school district. Working-class and poor white people aren't part of the debate except when the cops are being blamed for something.

Mom switches sides as much as she used to switch boyfriends, and as passionately, too. Just like everybody else, she complains about Jew landlords raising prices while lowering housing standards. If I point out that the boarded monstrosity around the corner is owned by an O'Reilly, she insists that he's only the front man. Landlords are all-powerful, vengeful, withholding Semitic gods who justify abandoning their responsibilities with claims they are controlled by stronger forces in the universe: unions, rent control, mortgage rates and thugs masquerading as community organizers.

But at the same time Mom's spitting with anger about experienced Jewish teachers being pushed out of their jobs in Brownsville because they dare to protect themselves from disruptive minority kids who are ruining everyone's education. For community leaders to claim that middle-class behavioral standards are racist attempts at controlling spirited black kids strikes her as a strategy for gaining power at the expense of all children. Mom is outraged at the rumor that some children and parents have yelled at Jewish teachers that they should have been made into lampshades, that it's too bad the genocide did not succeed. She stomps on the floor. "Nothing justifies that!"

All my best teachers are Jewish. It's Jewish teachers who confront Jewish kids for racist attitudes when we talk about the Civil War, civil rights or the Harlem Renaissance. How is it their fault that black kids score too low for the honors classes? How is it their fault that there aren't enough black teachers in the schools? At the same time, it's true, there are a lot of Jewish teachers in the system, and they haven't sweated about the dropout rate of poor and black and Puerto Rican kids. Some teachers, Jewish and Christian, are racist and fan the flames of hate smoldering in the city's schools.

I can't sleep at night. The past three years have been dedicated to graduating in June 1969 and here I am in November 1968 unable to go to classes. The papers continually recalculate makeup days and the point of no return that guarantees over one million kids will have to repeat a year. Then, finally, the strike is settled, with terms that are of no interest to us. Returning to school, even anticipating makeup days stretching to the summer, I want to kiss all my teachers and bring them flowers in celebration of being able to graduate after all.

Several days after Thanksgiving I agree to join Joan on a mission of mercy. We bundle up, prepared to walk across town carrying a cooler of turkey and fixings. Because she scored a twenty-eight-pound bird from a Catholic church, Mom waited for the day after Thanksgiving to buy another one, on sale. "This turkey has Jackie and Martin written on it," she warned us. Once it defrosted in the fridge, she roasted it, along with potatoes, yams and stuffing. She carved it, even though that task always reminds her there's no man around to help. Distraught that Jackie, worn out by her finicky husband and her colicky baby, didn't make it to the house for the holiday, Mom is determined that her first married daughter will enjoy a Thanksgiving meal and leftovers. Keeping one serving of white meat and dark meat for us, she wrapped up the rest of the turkey, recollecting other Thanksgivings while she stretched the A&P plastic wrap as tightly as she could without tearing. "Remember when we had two gay couples and Lacey tricked us into eating hash brownies?" She rhapsodizes about guests we barely knew but bites her tongue if anyone mentions Thanksgiving with my dad, who could eat an entire pumpkin pie by himself.

We happily sniff the food, but we don't want to barrel through the streets trailing the scent of turkey, sausage and cloves. Mom promises the smell will evaporate as soon as we are out and about in the cold. It could have been worse, she reminds us: "If I hadn't carved, you'd be pitching a bird over your shoulder in a knapsack, like a peasant from the old country."

"Which one?"

"Any old country."

We feel like any old delivery boys when we arrive at Jackie's. Not so much as a "Happy Thanksgiving" comes out of her mouth. All we get is "Hi kids."

We've never visited her apartment before, so we timidly navigate through the dark foyer to the kitchen. Jackie just nods in the direction of the kitchen: "Help yourselves."

As it turns out, there's nothing there to help ourselves to but beer and formula. It's as if she's doing us a favor by letting us fill up her fridge. Marriage hasn't changed her, I'm thinking, until my eyes adjust to the darkness. Jackie looks awful. Her hair is matted and she's wearing a stained empire dress that's too small for the belly of a new mom. Her face is covered with acne.

Baby Lisa is not looking much better. When we turn on the light near the crib, we cringe at the rash running all the way down the inside of her left leg. Joan swallows her own vomit as she points to the yellowish shit caked along the sides of the bars of the crib.

The plot thins. Now we know why Mom insisted on us bringing over the turkey. She's made it known that her days of cleaning up after babies are over. Now she's doling out yet another chance for us to learn about the drudgery that was her life for decades. Mom sweeps together all references to the past with "for decades" and "for too many years to count."

"For too many years to count, I waited for your father to

return." And then there's a story inevitably missing some crucial details.

"For decades I thought I would lose my mind." But then she offers no information about when that period ended.

She has no patience for our silly questions. I ask, "How old was I when my tonsils were removed?" and "What year did Ralph's hair burst into flames?" and she grouses she'd need her own secretary to retrace the calendars of our lives. Joan thinks I don't get an answer because of the way I ask; I think I don't get any answers because no one else will ask for me.

Now Jackie ignores Joan's question: "How often are you bathing Lisa and using Vaseline?"

When I ask Jackie if she'd mind if Joan cleaned up, she doesn't even get the joke. She just waves her arms as if she is the queen of the barn: "Help yourselves."

So we do. Noticing the pile of sleeveless 45s, we play "I Want to Hold Your Hand" three times. Joan beats out my effort to make Lisa gurgle happily, so I'm the one who has to clean the bath basin and heat up water for scrubbing the crib.

As if she was commenting on the weather, Jackie informed us: "Not a drop of hot water for days."

That's the kind of thing that would have made her rip shit with attitude a year ago. But now she sits on the couch staring at some awful fate as if it's someone else's life she doesn't have the energy to reject.

Jackie rouses herself once Lisa and the crib are clean. "How cold is it? Maybe we can get her outside for a bit. I need some cigs anyway."

Joan wins again. "It's not that cold," she says. "I'll help you with the stroller while Mary straightens up."

While they are out and about, I begrudgingly Mr. Clean the living room and kitchen, drawing the line at the bathroom. I'm relieved that Jackie had crooked a finger at the bedroom door: "That's none of your business." I peep inside only to see their messy waterbed reflected in an overhead mirror and a smashed vanity mirror shedding glass all over the floor.

When I reach for an ashtray under the couch in the living room, I'm surprised to discover a stash of *Playboy* magazines. I thought men didn't need them once they fell under the spell of the magic wand that transforms them into husbands.

It takes fifteen minutes just to clean the ashtrays. At least there's a roll of kitchen trash bags for the pizza boxes; Chinese takeout cartons; crumpled Lucky Strike, Marlboro, Winston and Newport Menthol packs; half-empty and empty cans of Bud, some of them with butts crushed and tilted on top; tissues spotted with blood; and two shit-encrusted, unsalvageable cloth diapers.

I cram three bags full, imagining Joan and me hauling them over our shoulders back home, banging on the door, and running away from our marked packages: "To: Sandy / From: The Old Country." But that would be too long a trip for such a short laugh.

Once I turn on more lights and remove the debris, the dirt becomes more visible. I'm not sure what makes me want to cry more: the work ahead of me or this view of Jackie's marriage. Even I didn't guess it would go downhill this fast.

When Jackie and Joan finally return with red-cheeked Lisa, I greet them like a perky maid: "Jackie, you wouldn't happen to have a vaccum cleaner hidden behind your secret door, would you?" I expect them to notice the improved order and odor. With the ashtrays emptied and the windows cracked open, the place seems half decent. The crib and coffee table shine, but neither one of my sisters gleams in return at me.

Instead Jackie announces: "Head home right now, before it gets any darker. Black kids are rampaging all over the city."

Joan suggests that we listen to the news first.

I'm relieved to hear Jackie sounding like herself again: "What's the matter with you? You didn't hear what those ladies said?"

Word is that some strike got out of control. Hundreds of black kids have attacked whites and Hispanics in schools and terrorized the subways.

I know it's serious when Jackie calls a cab.

"Wait a minute. What about you and Lisa?" I can tell by the way she asks that Joan still hasn't posed the million-dollar question: Where's Martin?

"We're staying. There are bars on the window and the double bolt is one of the few things that works in this dive." Jackie looks at me for the first time since I arrived. "Hey, cheer up. Husbands and wives fight. I knew he wasn't a prince. I just didn't know he wanted to live in a locker room. Two nights ago I threw him and his buddies out for treating the place like a motel. Haven't seen him or heard from him since. But, believe me, making up will be sweet."

During the cab ride home, I wonder: what's it going to take to make up with black people? Speaking into his rearview mirror, the black cabbie smiles at us. "You girls are lucky we're still

214

picking people up tonight. I wouldn't drive in Brooklyn even if you tipped me triple."

I figure he's worried that, because we're young, we'll forget to tip him. Mom's waitressing days taught us always to tip; we know that's what feeds the kids. I just hope he isn't one of those black people who thinks all white people are rich, because then he'll resent only ten percent. I'm examining the meter as if it's the EKG of a heart-attack victim. It would be a shame to end up dead broke and be forced to stiff the guy.

When he spots our building, the cabbie volunteers to watch us walk through the outside door after securing our promise that there's an adult waiting at home. I wish I could hand him five bucks and a photo of Martin with a message on the back: *If you see this turkey, please deliver to 46 Tremont Street, Apt. 1B.*

Upstairs, Mom, Alice and Ralph are glued to the radio. "Thank God you're home safe! Haven't you heard what's happening? I would never have sent you girls out today if I had known." Mom pokes at her glasses and hair. "Of all the nights for the antenna to conk out on us." Poker-faced newscasters disappear in a blizzard of horizontal buzzing lines before briefly returning to the screen. Even the TV knows there's too much chaos for straightforward, droning reportage.

We learn in bits and pieces that black kids have taken to the streets as part of the Citywide Student Strike Committee. Mom challenges us, as if we control some inside track on the news, "I wanna know who is giving these kids these ideas? Who is egging them on to do what they don't dare do themselves?"

Alice tells us that nothing but the usual fights happened at her school and I add that I heard only the typical cursing and yelling in the halls when I switched classes. Joan doesn't have to pipe in. We all know that her College-Bound program is insulated from the rest of her school in order to peacefully conduct its experiment in transforming underachievers into leaders.

Then we hear a loud gurgling sound coming from Alice's bedroom. Realizing that Ralph has left the living room, we scramble to see what's up. Emma first, as usual. She never passes up a chance to bounce toward novelty.

Mom squeezes past Emma to approach Ralph. "You know better than that. Hanging isn't something to joke about." Twisting to look at him closely with her good eye, she tries not to lose her temper. "What did you do to Emma's monkey, you little pisser?"

Remnants of a snake knotted to a monkey tail are wrapped around his neck and stretched upward. Ralph balances on one leg on top of a dresser, holding his other leg back and up, almost as high as the arm from which he dangles his rope of fur. The room is littered with indications that he has reacted to the news of the day by eviscerating the three stuffed animals the kids brought back from their last trip to the Bronx Zoo.

Ralph howls as he swiftly kicks out the one leg he is standing on and lands in an open drawer with the other. He challenges Mom: "Is this funny?" As the drawer breaks and he crashes down, he kicks her in the shoulder so hard, she knocks down Emma as she falls backward. He keeps kicking until the sides of the drawer are flattened. Then he hurls the severed head of Emma's monkey at her. Pieces of snipped parrot litter Alice's bed, but she doesn't notice because she is preoccupied by staring at the rest of her parrot, impaled on the curtain-rod brackets.

Mom stays calm. She's in genuine emergency mode. "Let me talk to him alone."

She nods when I mouth "Lacey?" on my way out the door. We howl for Lacey to join us from Queens only in crisis, and this counts.

Over the next two hours, Joan and I stay tuned to radio warnings about bottle- and rock-hurling young black men attacking police and innocent bystanders in subways. At the same time, we listen to the curdling and banging noises seeping from Alice's room. We cry when finally we hear Ralph and Mom sobbing together.

I remember Ralph's odd behavior the day the kids picked their sacrificial stuffed animals at the Bronx Zoo. When strangers stared at Emma's expert mimicking of monkey sounds and motions, she blushed, encouraged by the attention. Ralph shook his fists at them and yelled, "You leave my sister alone." They laughed, oblivious that he perceived them as threatening rather than friendly. Resigned to his antagonistic posturing, as if that's the way boys are, we didn't even ask Ralph to stop or explain that folks were well-intentioned. We were just grateful when he finally relaxed and, by the end of the day, wrapped his snake around his neck in gleeful imitation of Emma flaunting her bushy monkey tail as if it were a mink stole.

Now I think he harbored a vexed relationship with those stuffed animals from the time they were selected, as though they had tricked him into participating in the family. Only eight years old, he flails at others when he regrets a choice he has made. He often regrets cooperation with us, as though it compromises his capacity to be a boy. Staying separate is his only hope; otherwise he might go crazy unraveling the whirling mix of reverence and contempt for men that have always circulated in our house. Neither strikes nor negotiated settlements will help this city and its many families resolve the crises of so many disadvantaged, disruptive boys.

28

SEX AND THE INNER CITY

"Hush up everyone. Jackie has an announcement to make."

Accepting Mom's cue, everyone except Ralph and I grin in anticipation, sure Jackie is going to proclaim another pregnancy. Instead, she manages to surprise all of us by choking on her words. "Martin and I are separating temporarily. Just to sort things out. I'm gonna live here for a while so that Mom can take care of Lisa while I work."

"Don't sweat it, Mary. Nothing you can do. It's her business," Joan advises me, as she does more and more often. We share a bed, but we hardly see each other anymore and I guess she needs independence from me as much as I need mine from Mom. Now that a girl named Juanita is Joan's best friend, she shares decisions with me, not doubts and questions.

For instance, "Mount Holyoke is out for all of us" is what she concluded out of the blue a week after she returned from her all-expense-paid tour of campuses. The girls in the College-Bound program bonded over rejecting Mount Holyoke. "These chicks serving tea and wearing white gloves were so out of it, they didn't understand our accents. Two of the princesses couldn't believe I lived where I said," Joan complained. Full scholarship or not, she's not applying to any place prissy.

It's ironic that there are programs to help kids who fail but not those who succeed moderately. Joan flubbed a couple of years instead of steadily chugging along like me, so she has had more opportunities and developed more friendships with like-minded people because she was placed in the College-Bound program. I still think about the national fitness audit in ninth-grade P.E. when everyone had to hit a tennis ball across the net three times. Those of us who swung adequately at the first round of five balls that the rented machine chugged at us were sidelined the rest of the period while the less coordinated kept trying. I practiced swinging a racket four times; the uncoordinated got twenty opportunities. I'm itching to wrap my hands around a tennis racket again and to feel that satisfying *ping* of a ball flying off the strings.

Mom is pleased at Joan's rejection of the hoity-toity place and somewhat mollified by my applying to the College of Mount Saint Vincent and the University of Dayton. If I'm going away, it might as well be a Catholic college, she says. I'm confident I'll be admitted to both places; it's the financial aid packages I'll hear about soon that worry me. Although she disagrees with my choice only to apply to two colleges and not to pursue what she calls a competitive liberal arts college, the counselor still pokes me in the shoulder when she sees me in the hall: "You're going to college, remember that!" She doesn't know me well enough to get over her concern that I'll jump into marriage.

Joan's on a first-name basis with her counselor, who once again encourages her to work at a city camp this coming summer. Under Joan's watchful eyes, Ralph and Alice will ride air-conditioned buses to Bear Mountain for free; take swimming lessons in big, clean pools; and not fret about money when selecting construction paper and iridescent Magic Markers for arts and crafts projects. Joan considers herself part of Mayor Lindsay's efforts to help disadvantaged kids, so she politely challenges Mom for reciting one of the rampant rhymes of the day: "John Lindsay, Master of the Bungle; He turned New York into a Jungle."

Today, Mom, on behalf of Jackie, instigates a debate with Joan. "You're allowed to be a counselor because the pay stinks, but a white girl like Jackie can't get any of the plum jobs in the antipoverty programs. Minimum wage is all she's going to get."

Jackie doesn't waste her energy on these arguments; she's into family politics. "Don't worry about me. My man is headed for a union job and will take care of me and Lisa just fine." No one but Jackie believes they will reunite. Waking up in the middle of the night, heart pounding, she's the kind of person who tells herself the scurrying sound is her upstairs neighbor's cat, not mice or rats.

With premeditated casualness Joan reminds Mom that a lot of black people with high school diplomas couldn't get a minimum-wage job as fast as Jackie did. Then she catches herself: "Jackie, of course, I wish you didn't have to be a cashier."

Joan gets part of her wish. Jackie doesn't work as a cashier for long. Three days after reporting to work, she comes home blustering about the assholes and the crappy machines. Lulu this and Joey that. Nasty, na-a-sty customers. Slammed by her supervisor for scamming too many bathroom and cigarette breaks, she quit.

Initially Mom was counting on rent and baby-sitting money from Jackie, but two weeks of watching a baby cured her grandmother illusions. She'd rather go back to being on call at the two candy stores that slip her money off the books for working the counters when no family member can cover. Mom says she'd love to step into the cashier job Jackie just blew. With a salary plus welfare, she could handle a three-bedroom in a better neighborhood. But welfare benefits are zapped as soon as you work a regular job.

If Jackie moves home more permanently, we'll all go crazy. Jackie is a human chimney and a whiz at creating clutter. A half hour after she arrives home, an empty kitchen table resembles a flea market stand. If Alice or Ralph are even five minutes late when they are scheduled to watch Lisa, Jackie yells at them until they cry. She'll claim to have missed appointments in order to leverage maximum guilt. Her unhappiness is a vacuum into which she sucks others to keep herself from being too lonely.

At first when Jackie returned home, the supply of sympathy was endless. It was appalling that Martin stayed out all night with the boys and treated folks to a round of drinks when the refrigerator at home was nearly empty.

"Men are no good," Mom said.

"Lazy motherfuckas they always turn out to be."

"They never amount to much."

"No more of this Frankenstein Be My Valentine."

"Good thing Martin left you with only one kid."

After living with Jackie for a month, we realize that Martin probably has a story to tell, too. If not for us, Lisa would live in virtual solitary confinement, stuck alone behind the bars of her crib sucking bottles of sugar water. When Jackie complains about taking care of one kid, Mom grumbles, "She isn't even working, for Christ's sake."

One day Mom blows up. "You've always been a lazy bitch—except when it comes to causing trouble."

"Where do you think I learned to be a bad mother? I got knocked up just to get away from you."

Without drawing close enough to touch, they threaten each other with familiar household weapons: the broom, a frying pan and a lamp. But neither one launches a missile. Their battle is a charade, a farcical reenactment of past skirmishes. We are robots, programmed to repeat the routine motions of relationships.

Jackie's fight with a woman who lives downstairs, on the other hand, is the real thing. One Tuesday, Guadalupe comes home from work with a pounding period-migraine, seeking some peace and quiet before her kids return from school, and instead finds her boyfriend José drinking beer and laughing with Jackie.

Guadalupe's screams of "puta" lure half our neighbors into the hall in time to spy Jackie leaving, her blouse ripped open and a patch of hair missing. Later on we would see the welts on her back, but at first everyone assumed Jackie whupped Guadalupe, whose face was bloodied.

But Guadalupe definitely won the honor war. After broadcasting how she came home sick to find her man with a white puta, she paraded through the halls with the bouquets José brought her. He might be unemployed, but at least José started working overtime to make Guadalupe happy again: picking up the kids after school, grocery shopping, and foot massages every night for a week. "He even cleans and sucks my toes," she boasted, so that Jackie could hear.

Jackie doesn't dare retort in public as she does at home: "He has no other place to go, so he has to keep his fat mama happy." She insists that she and José weren't doing anything. "How could people believe he was feeling me up? They all saw me get my ass out of there with my bra in place!"

It's a relief to all of us when Martin starts calling every night. He's looking better to us and to her all the time.

I remind everyone I'm never going to get married.

"Me neither," Ralph says.

Joan changes the tune: "I'm going to marry the right man."

"Good luck finding him," says Mom.

Joan, Alice and I make a list of all the men in the building. About every third family has one. If they work, most of them do so at night. Some of the women put up with certified creeps and madmen who have disability payments because of Vietnam or an accident on the job. Only two of the couples in the building pass for happy, but Joan insists, loud enough for Ralph to hear, that there are a lot of good men out there. We want him to know about men who stick it out through the hard times—even if we've never personally met one. Maybe we should also make more of an effort to educate Emma about men and decency.

At the age of five, Emma already enters a room armed with radar for attention. Tall for her age, with long thick platinum blond hair just like her unmentionable father's, Jackie's old boyfriend, she struts into the living room, all smiles. As the baby of the family, she's used to having an audience, but always looks for new recruits. Especially if there's a man around, she has taken to punctuating her entrance by prancing and giggling. "Want to see my zipper?"

Some people refuse to follow her cue, teasing her by saying no or showing her some quirk about one of their own zippers. Not the guy visiting today, whom we sometimes call Henry and sometimes Henrietta, depending on how he is dressed. He knows how to encourage a performance.

Imitating the moves of a stripper, Emma quickly but smoothly rolls her shirt so that it stays in place in the middle of her chest. Twirling a couple of times while pulling down her panties, she expertly wiggles out of them, tilts to the side and makes sure our guest enjoys a full view of the zipper that starts on her lower back and stretches across the left cheek of her butt.

A scar that size on such a gorgeous kid could make people feel sad, except that Emma doesn't seem to mind. She celebrates it and invites others to do the same. With pride she launches into the story of how a rusted blade of a sled loosened and then hooked her butt as she sped downhill in a snowstorm, tingling with numbness from the cold that muted the sensation of flesh ripping. After her accident she limped two blocks home with Ralph without shedding a tear.

Next, Emma strips off her shirt in order to expose another magnificent scar, secured when she was only three. Trying to pull on mom's sleeve to steal her attention while she sat talking at the kitchen table, Emma snagged the tablecloth instead. As she yanked, a pot of hot coffee came down on her, scalding her upper arm. The mottled, elongated oval shape of the permanent burn scar resembles an overcooked, shriveled hot dog.

Even though it's chilly, Emma remains in the state of undress her tale of her scars seems to require. Once she visibly shivers, she climbs up on Henry's lap, obliging him to wrap his arms around her and rock her. If she is following her usual pattern, pretty soon she will call him Daddy.

The spectacle makes me feel nauseous. My littlest sister has absorbed the grooming for being sexy. Doesn't my mother see that Emma's provocative performances foreshadow that she will be a flirt like Jackie, always searching for an intoxicating amalgam of fun and father figures?

"How did Emma learn to do such a thing?" I quizzed my mother the first time I witnessed a performance, expecting her to share my alarm.

"Don't be such a spoilsport," she chided. "Emma's just a little girl having fun, something you've never understood."

I slumped away, dejected again. Yet I am still clumsily courting my mother after all these years. She is my first unrequited love, and someone I suspect I will always misunderstand as much as she fails to comprehend me. I want to give up on her like a landlord who is no longer committed to repairing damage caused by careless tenants. But I can't. It's through censored exchanges with her that I define myself.

Mom, you're right. I don't value fun. I'm after pleasure. Fun is belly laughs and silly rhymes, like "See ya later, masturbater." Dancing in a line with you, Joan and Alice, pretending we are the Supremes, is fun. Basketball is fun, except when the few nasty girls threaten me for guarding too close or playing too well: "You'll be sorry for putting your smelly breath in my face" or "You make another basket and I'll break your wrists." Being the only white girl on the gym floor is not fun, but running and sweating until it is time to slow down and focus on that hoop replaces my grimace with a grin. Being a five-year-old stripper isn't fun; it's sick.

Pleasure is what I do alone that cannot be spoken about without shocking other people, even my best friends. Everyone talks about boys jerking off, shooting their stuff, coming all over the place, which sounds like the kind of fun you have when you turn on a fire hydrant on a hot night. But no one talks about this dreamy state in which I press my hips down on the bed or arch under the bathroom faucet until the thrumming between my legs makes me breathe and clench, breathe and clench, finally feeling such a sweet ease in my belly. It's the same kind of pleasure that bursts inside me when I suddenly understand a poem or see, with unusual vividness, the unique beauty of an object, like a tree in morning light. At the annual school trip to an art museum I've learned to break away, let a painting draw me to it, and then discreetly perform a slow cha-cha as I assess how far away from it I should stand, poised for it to come alive. Noticing details in a painting adjusts my vision so that I can observe objects and people with more clarity than usual. I stop feeling anxious and drift into contentment. Fun is social, energetic and fleeting; pleasure is solitary, spatial and also fleeting.

29

ENVELOPES

Receiving bulky manila envelopes in the mail usually makes me feel sophisticated, but right now I'd settle for simple relief. Based on what the admissions officer from the University of Dayton said on the phone, today's package should lift the load I've carried since talking to a dean at the College of Mount Saint Vincent last week. In five minutes I sank from her warm congratulations on my admission to her curtly informing me, "The decision is final." My financial aid package would generously cover tuition, books and fees, but I should live at home rather than seek funding for room and board. "You're only sixteen," she reminded me, in a tone of voice that implied I had forgotten about crucial extenuating circumstances such as a criminal record or debilitating disease.

I immediately called Dayton, the other school I applied to, and was quickly put through to the person who had sold me on the place. Last spring, at the one-day college fair I attended for only a half hour after classes because I needed to hustle to work, I quickly scanned the gym for the shortest lines. I used the strategy that worked beautifully at the 1964 World's Fair, where I entered the Sudan pavilion because there was no wait and no fee, and was granted an hourlong conversation with a black man who spoke English with a British accent and was fluent in French and two native dialects, but still took me, a twelve-year-old, seriously. He allowed me to leaf through huge picture books even though I was upfront in explaining I couldn't purchase anything. For days afterward I thought about civil war and famine against the backdrop of a lush landscape, knowing I would never again imagine his continent as merely a massively expanded version of the African habitat at the Bronx Zoo.

The alumnus at an ignored table representing the University of Dayton was similarly eye-opening. This was a Catholic college I hadn't heard of before. He testified that his excellent education and residential experience led him to choose a career encouraging more high school students from the East Coast to attend. In response to my 88 average, test scores and preference for a quiet campus, he beamed: "Unless you're a discipline problem, which I doubt, you'll get in for sure." My financial situation did not dissuade him at all, quite the opposite. He deftly explained various federal programs and the college's policy of distributing full scholarships to highly qualified kids in order to improve regional representation. I accepted the application form and fat catalog from him as if they were a gift.

On the phone last week, this guy enthusiastically congratulated me on my admission and described me to prove he remembered who I was. "We think you're an excellent fit for our institution, and I'm sure you'll be pleased with the financial aid package, which should be mailed early next week." When I rip open my package now in the hall outside the mailboxes, one detail in it flashes like a sordid neon light: "Federal Loan: $2,300." I focus on other details at each stair landing after first checking the corners where trouble might lurk. Recently someone was mugged on the second floor an hour after she cashed her check, before she bought even a smidgen of food for her three kids. I feel mugged, too.

The congratulatory cover letter mentions a full scholarship, but finally it dawns on me that during my few stolen hours of reading catalog explanations of financial aid I had made a mistake as gargantuan as substituting a multiplication symbol for an addition sign. Maybe all schools are like the ones Mrs. Brustein recommended before losing patience with me. Unless you are a brilliant student or athlete, you have to borrow money. She probably assumed everyone knows that the term "full scholarship" can be used to refer only to tuition, like Sears advertising in large print a half-price washer and adding in small print that the customer must simultaneously purchase a full-price dryer.

I hadn't focused on the specifics of college applications as much as other kids in my classes. They talked endlessly about their brothers' and sisters' experiences, quotas against Jewish people and who helped them with essays. Now I'm paying for feigning indifference while obsessing about small details. Two catalogs mentioned that generally freshman work-study entails assignments in the cafeteria. I had no intention of wearing hairnets and rubber gloves, so I ruled those schools out and, as if nothing else mattered, stayed on red alert for signs of which colleges required dining-hall service.

I had been shocked to realize that many scholarships require maintaining a 3.0 or 3.5 average. That could mean trouble for me: my grades appear and shrink as mysteriously as pimples. I got a 99 on the Geometry Regent's exam but only a 540 on the math PSAT. Reviewing Spanish in class the day before an exam, I know every answer before someone else shouts it out. The day of an exam, my conjugations and accents inexplicably misbehave, tearing up fifteen points. If a kid in class asks how I did after a test, I say "more than a C for sure," hedging my bets against humiliation and disappointment. After I scrutinized the fine print about scholarships, I worried if money had to be returned when a scholarship is canceled because of poor grades. That's when I decided to ignore Mrs. Brustein and only apply to schools where I was above average and would for sure be courted.

I'm warding off the nagging feeling that I should have accepted her coaching when the deadlines for college and scholarship applications started popping up with the unpredictability of a softball pitch rather than the regularity of tennis balls spat out by a machine. I plausibly imitated the proper stance at bat, but I scrunched my eyes as the ball hurtled toward me. Ducking harder decisions, I applied only to the two peaceful Catholic schools I felt connected to and confident would welcome me unconditionally, without loans.

Dayton loses all of its luster now that I dread sinking into a lifetime of debt before I graduate. Why live in Ohio, a daylong bus ride away from friends and family, unable to return for Thanksgivings? Regret darkens my mood for days until I swallow my pride and turn to my only hope. Penitent for not listening and desperate for attention, I burst into Mrs. Brustein's office. "Because I didn't listen to you, I can't go to college after all."

She laughs at my long face and puts her arm around me. "Do you think you're the only one of the six hundred I'm responsible for who doesn't listen to me?" Not once does she say "I told you so." Instead she offers, "There's more than one way to skin a cat. Don't accept or reject Dayton until we talk again. Now scoot. You have classes and I have work to do."

Mrs. Brustein couldn't break through my stubborn wall of ignorance about choosing where to apply to college. I had completed my applications as if they were for temporary employment rather than four years of education. Only three major principles motivated me: avoiding riots, loans and home. Make that one principle: avoidance. I am adamant in my refusals and haphazard in my embraces. Yet she puts my file on top of the snowdrift of paper on her desk.

Two weeks later my distant, weary homeroom teacher raises eyebrows by calling me to the front of the room, handing over an envelope with a letter folded inside, and saying, "You're excused from all your classes today if that's what it takes." I've been summoned to Mrs. Brustein's office, where there's a stack of paper and another handwritten note from my counselor. "Mary, start filling these out immediately. Don't leave without seeing me." At the bottom of the stack I find photocopies of my two other applications for admissions and financial aid. This is the kind of forethought and organization expected of executive secretaries. I am duly impressed and brimming with gratitude as I finally follow her lead although I've never heard of the school to which I am now applying on a form stamped RUSH.

As soon as her first appointment leaves her office, Mrs. Brustein barges out and commands me, "Get in here." I smile; belatedly I understand she's brusque because she's busy. She hurriedly tells me that a newly accredited school in Westchester County, soon to disaffiliate with the Catholic Church, is particularly eager to identify high-achieving poor kids from public high schools; I am a shoo-in even applying late. She has already shown the admissions people my record. "Until the rest of the nuns move out, there's no dorm space, so you'll get to live as you wish."

This is what it is like to have insiders pull strings for you: within ten days of applying I receive word of a full tuition scholarship and a stipend for off-campus housing. With scholarship in hand and a debt-free future, I can finally tell my family and friends that I'm going to a small college in Westchester County not far from the Hudson River. Joan and Mom hug and kiss me. If I announced my engagement to someone they never heard me mention before, I'd be bombarded with questions. But even curiosity about guys usually peters out before we focus on what's best for us. We count ourselves lucky if someone or something chooses us. Selectivity is for other people, and for snobs.

Carol and Ann balk at my spilling over in excitement on the train ride to Rockaway Friday night after work. I'm tired and wired. Carol's just tired as she says, "I still don't get it. It's not like you're gonna be a doctor or anything."

"I know I can be an executive secretary without a degree, but first I'm taking a long vacation of uninterrupted reading," I say glibly. I hint at nothing about the inexplicable desire to be like my supervisor at the Trim the Tree Shop at Altman's who spontaneously talked for thirty minutes about cherubs after he overheard me calling them naked angels. Without turning over a card to read the small print, he could identify the titles of the paintings and the names of the painters on the museum Christmas cards we handed to customers who spent over a hundred dollars.

It's putting off earning a living that stumps Carol, especially because she knows that just like her I'm eager to have my own place. She wants a house, matching furniture and increasingly visible respectability. I want the aura of legitimacy a B.A. bestows. Carol works in order to succeed. I work in order to pass over into a world where leisure and dreaming are possible. I imagine college as a state of being and an absence of the life I have known; it is as amorphous and tantalizing an ideal as heaven.

My friends and I are better off sticking to short-term thinking. Collectively complaining about living at home this summer, we hatch a plan. They are starting full-time, permanent secretarial jobs in Manhattan after graduation but wouldn't mind traveling back and forth to Rockaway if we can find an affordable rental.

Sunday morning at the boarding house where we frequently stay, our landlady rattles off names of summer landlords. We're slightly daunted to learn that lower monthly rates for two-bedroom cottages with outdoor showers are contingent on three-month leases. The landlord of the place we prefer won't budge, but he gives us a week to commit. Drawn to the flower boxes on each windowsill and the way the cottage is recessed away from the street, by Thursday we decide to skip graduation ceremonies and move out to Rockaway in mid-June to make paying the extra month's rent worthwhile.

I conjure twenties tucked in books and coat pockets to pay my $120 for first-month rent and damage deposit and then secure them throughout my body in case I'm mugged on the train. After the landlord accepts Carol's and Ann's two checks, he gingerly counts the rumpled bills I've flattened against each other in an envelope, as if he knows they were smuggled to Rockaway in my socks and bra. Mom never had a checking account, but I'm getting one as soon as I start college.

When I breezily mention my summer plans to my mom, she flicks a wobbly cigarette ash at my chest. "Good riddance to you, then. You're so eager to get out of here, you might as well take all your stuff with you and head for college straight from the beach." I've caught her on the wrong day, once again.

Our fights resemble a slide machine wildly clicking the same scene from different angles. Sometimes it looks like I'm winning, sometimes losing. During this tiff I try to assume the role of referee, cajoling my own outraged self and jealous mother into behaving ourselves. Although I want to scream about how unfair it is to punish me for getting what she never had, instead I haggle with her; "I need to leave stuff here and you need evidence that I live here to keep the welfare money for me coming through August." We're as practical as we are passionate in our arguments, and easily shift to the next slide.

"Fine, but I'm not running a flophouse. I want all those clothes and books out of here in September. I'm not gonna be stuck hauling them when I find a better place." She's stopped being punitive and has returned to dreaming about moving away from the park. Her gain will be my loss and vice versa. In the struggle for the survival of the fittest, even mother and daughter are pitted against one another.

30

DEAD MAN'S FLOAT

Ann is everybody's friend but nobody's girlfriend, so neither Carol nor I can bring our boyfriends to the cottage for make-out sessions. That suits us just fine. It would be harder to control them there. Among ourselves we call them "dateboys" and "foreigners"—creatures with Roman hands and Russian fingers.

Sometimes Carol and Ann turn on me because of my college plans: "You're the one who is Roman and Russian away." The fact that I chose a small college in Westchester County rather than going farther away doesn't appease them, as I had hoped. They act as if I'm about to be locked up in a convent far away from their world. We avoid the topic most of the time, determined to enjoy our summer living together.

In Rockaway, John and I settle into a Friday and Saturday night routine. The fake ID he scored for me opens doors so that I can join him for beers in any bar he chooses. Usually Ann goes with me so that we can dance. If she doesn't show, I amuse John by dancing by myself. I now understand the appeal of bars: they promote sexual bonding by hindering conversation. John doesn't dance, even slow, except lying down. In his car we figure out how to move like we were made for each other. People say "you suck" as if it's gross, but I discover the bliss of returning again and again to the same spots on his neck, drawing on the skin, while I clasp one of his legs between mine. He thinks it's cute until his friends start teasing him about all the hickeys and asking what else he's getting off me.

I believe him when he promises me he tells them, "None of your business." He certainly doesn't tell them about my rule: "I'm not going to waste my life going below the waist." He doesn't push or beg as aggressively as his brother Larry does with Carol, but one night I ruin everything by praising him once too often: "You're going to be one of those cops who follows the rules instead of going off doing whatever you want." I should know better than praising a guy for being good; even John takes it as a challenge to prove he's an outlaw. He explains why he puts up with me leaving him with blue balls: he's getting plenty on the side.

A chick with a baby and a husband who works nights makes no demands on him except that he bring his own rubbers and remember to leave with them. "She wasn't hot for sex until after the baby, and her husband is not much interested in her now that she has the kid. I'm keeping this family together!"

Scenes of a burly man busting into the bedroom and strangling both of them crash through my brain. What if her husband finds out?

My heart races and eyes blur. "Don't you feel guilty about

betraying me? I'm not gonna be a warmup for another girl! You're an asshole, you know that?"

Unflappable as always, John describes his other girl, but won't tell me her name. My small tits are just fine, but her melons are luscious. Her hips and thighs are womanly. He complains that sometimes he has to readjust beneath me because my bony hips carve into his thighs clear through his jeans.

I've been thinking of John as a casual boyfriend, but the idea of him with another woman suddenly makes him seem essential. Love has finally made a dramatic appearance in my life. I can't sit back and let him sneak around because I'm holding out. Music courses through me: *He's so fine, tonight I'm gonna make him mine.*

This is what we have been warming up to all year. We dance in the back seat longer than usual, breaking the rules. His penis rises in my hands. I'm amazed that it can stick straight out and then bend so easily at different angles; it is soft and solid at the same time. He's the experienced one, but he's shy about what I notice and surprised by how I react. He slides his fingers into my wetness, and for the first time I know that my own hands are second best. My sensations are less intense but more diffuse without the interference of the seams of our jeans. At just the right moment, he touches me and I melt and giggle after several twitches and echoes. He giggles, too.

I'm dazed and barely know where I am. But when he takes out a rubber, I remember. "Not yet, next weekend." We agree we won't do it until we have some place other than the car. Sweet John wants my first time to be perfect.

Tuesday night when I'm at work, John leaves a sealed envelope under my door. The note reads, in big capital letters, HEY

BABY, FRIDAY NIGHTS' THE BIG NIGHT. I GOT KEYS TO DONNY'S PLACE. I'LL PICK YOU UP AT SEVIN.

But by then I have already decided to back out of my promise. All day Sunday, all day at work Monday and Tuesday, remembering our last night in the car, I devised a litany of complaints against him. I wasn't feeling love; the heat of jealousy, one of the seven deadly sins, had accelerated my heartbeat. John is a nice-enough guy, but he can't even spell. When I berate him for using words like "nigger," he retreats to smug silence. Straight-faced he told me his married lady's melons were luscious, as if he were reading a letter in *Playboy*. Words like "Negro" and "breasts" are too dignified for him. All his life, he'll go to the same bars and live in the same neighborhood. Even two years in the service didn't make him curious about the world.

Wednesday night, during my long train ride back to Rockaway from Manhattan, I wipe tears with my sleeves, saddened by thoughts I can't shake: I dote on him in the dark and look down on him in conversation. I wince at recollections of his staccato responses to my comments; to disguise having little to say, he acts as if I'm babbling. What I most like is the way he smells. Soap, beer, cigarettes, mint toothpaste, and whiskey zoom me elsewhere, into a zone of moisture, warmth and ease. When I'm away from him, I can't remember what he looks like; I can only remember how he awakens my body and exiles my worries.

Friday night looms. I had no choice but to face Cookie in the park, but now I have options. I'm running home for the weekend.

Instead of calling John from the corner pay phone, I beg Ann to remember to tape a sealed envelope to our door before she leaves Friday night. "Something is up at home. I may not be able to reach John and don't want him waiting for me when I'm all the way in the Bronx. Please, please remember he always knocks at the back door." Working as a saleslady has taught me devious courtesy.

In the note that I rewrite four times, I lie to John. *I made a vow to keep my virginity until college; I'm sorry for being such a tease. Let's go back to the no-play-below-the-waist rule.* I crumple and toss the draft in which I break up with him.

Home now for the first time in six weeks, I know keeping my virginity was the right decision even though there's an achy fullness in my stomach and I'm throbbing between my legs. I crave John. My values have become vague and my appetites sharp.

As a kid, I expected to pursue pure thoughts when I grew up, to spend hours on scientific principles and poetic, noble phrases. Instead I'm most aware of clothes and what goes on underneath them. Is everyone this distracted by daytime dreams of sex, or am I particularly so, having been raised to both dread and desire men and romance as if they are an end in themselves? I practice being well-behaved at work, but in my social life I am most comfortable around booze and light sarcasm. I rarely remember to think about values and poetry anymore. Most of the time I am relieved simply to stay out of trouble and one step ahead of my obligations.

When I attended church as a child, I didn't question or affirm the existence of god. I simply believed I belonged in the expansive and quiet environs of pews, altars and richly carpeted aisles, where it seemed possible to be compassionate and contemplative. Now I stand on cracked, crumbling pavement in the middle of an unnamed intersection of influences where the light functions only occasionally. Alert for opportunity or danger from every direction, I jolt my attention to wherever there is honking and commotion, barely noticing streets where some calm vista has been preserved.

I desperately want to talk to Joan, but I'm asleep by the time she climbs into bed after seeing her boyfriend Friday and Saturday nights, and then I'm relieved that Sunday belongs to the kids. Sometimes responsibility for others is the only distraction that clears my head.

Ralph intends to prove that he can beat all of us at darts, and Alice, no longer expecting Mom to be her witness, wants me to applaud her swimming all the way across the Mullaly Park pool. The park is now quietly policed and Lindsay has pumped money into repairing the pool, Ping-Pong tables and table hockey area. Emma tags along today because she has missed Ralph and Alice all week when they were in camp, although she loves nothing better than playing with Mom in sight. Five and a half years old, Emma is still so close to Mom that she crawls in bed next to her many nights. They sink down in the center of the sofa bed, somehow sharing the hole they have created.

Ralph slugs the bull's-eye again and again. Holding his body and arm the same way each time, he looks so serious Emma can't stop giggling. Maybe he'll find a home in the military some day, because he clearly doesn't belong here. He's even serious in the pool. After Alice splashes her way across and Emma finds playmates in the shallow end, Ralph swims only a little and then gives up.

Joan watched him all summer at camp. She whispers, "He can't stick with anything he thinks he can't be great at. Failure makes him lose it. I have some scary stories to tell you." She pauses. "Even if there's funding next year, Ralph won't be allowed to enroll."

Ralph begins to float, rigidly holding his body on top, moved along very slowly by the motion of the water. When a group of kids splashes him, he stands up, says nothing, and then returns to floating, as if in a trance that yields indifference to the energy and attacks of others. The crawl and the sidestroke are too hard and he's fearful he might touch someone else. Ralph has perfected the dead man's float.

A woman next to us says sympathetically, "There's something wrong with that boy."

"We know. We know."

My heart flinches at the sight of my brother as a floating corpse. I wonder if that's what John is to me now, too.

I approached being a girlfriend as a job, like being a saleslady or a messenger. I grew up hearing about men using women, and I've seen plenty of evidence that they lay waste to our lives. But women, too, use men. I'm less flamboyantly obsessed with male attention than Emma and Jackie are, but I have to admit I yearned for someone unthreatening to nuzzle with. From the start I had restricted John to the dimensionality of a paper doll. At sweet sixteen, I'm packing a learner's permit for lust and a heap of dire warnings about relationships.

Eventually John and I talk briefly and shed each other as naturally as a snake sloughs off dead skin. We should have known all along we wouldn't last beyond the summer; maybe we did. What I couldn't have guessed is that I would lose Carol and Ann as well.

Boys think that the worst form of leading a guy on is making out without going all the way, leaving them with blue balls. Carol was concerned that I left John with a red face. I had given people the impression that I had a serious relationship with her fiancé's brother when I was actually treating him like a way station before a new life. I'm stung by the truth of her accusation but also struck by the cowardice of her claiming that's why she's ending our friendship. She's choosing Larry over me. Maybe there isn't a readily available script for explaining estrangement from me now that she's planning on marrying and moving to the suburbs while I go off to college. Ann, who was always the silent partner, follows Carol's lead.

Some days I feel abandoned and friendless, others I luxuriate in a sense of freedom: my friends have released me to become a college girl.

31

RAPPROCHEMENT

Like all first-year students, I move to college in a flurry. It takes three buses to arrive at my rented room in a private home, lugging everything I can in a battered suitcase and three big shopping bags. That was managed only after weeks of phone calls to coordinate the schedule for the city bus from the Bronx to Yonkers with the one that stops near the college. When I called the school for help, the nuns refused to believe that I knew absolutely no one with a car who would drive me to school. I still wince at the inexplicable gruffness with which Lacey refused: "I'm too busy." It takes me weeks to figure out that I have traveled only thirty miles from home. For those of us who measure distance by blocks and the trajectories of public transportation rather than the miles that cars traverse, I might as well be across the country. Welcome to Freshman Disorientation, I mutter, trying to be brave.

My room is bigger than I imagined and I share a bathroom

with only one other person. Once my scholarship money comes in, I'm going to be just fine, I tell myself, even if I don't have a family anymore. For a while Mom seemed reconciled to the idea of more education, but splitting for Rockaway for what was supposed to be my last summer at home made her angry at me again. On my way out the door to college, with most of my belongings bulging off my body like knots on a tree, she informed me I wasn't welcome back home in the same tone of voice she might use turning away a door-to-door salesman. There was no scene, just the announcement of my refugee status. I scribble curses on the blank wall of my brain that I run into when I find myself brooding about Joan, Alice, Ralph and Emma. I've wanted to be on my own for years, but I never intended to disappear or be exiled. I expected to have a chance to leave *and* to cleave.

After all of these years of striving to go to college, I have landed in a place that started awarding four-year degrees seven years ago and became fully accredited last year. It is the antithesis of Radcliffe and Columbia. I am a first-generation college student at a first-generation college. Everyone else at the school lives at home with their parents, except for the few Westchester County housewives pursuing college degrees now that their kids are grown. The fact that I walk three miles a day to and from school and flatly state that I can't afford a car or driving lessons sets me apart as much as the fact that I have moved to attend a mediocre commuter college.

I've been Miracle Whipped when I expected real mayonnaise. Even in college, most people aren't excited about ideas. Outside of class I'm teased for obsessing about my difficulties finishing a paper comparing Martin Buber's notion of the "I-Thou" relationship to Picasso's representations of how we are three- and four-faced, and thus slated for prismatic complexity interacting with others. Several teachers drop hints that I would have no trouble transferring to a better school. When I explain my scholarship and aversion to debt, they reply that practically everyone borrows to attend college, as if no one should refuse a common fate.

For a couple of weeks, I try to bribe my way into friendships, even using my most perfect handwriting to copy my scribbled-but-thorough notes for one guy who thanks me profusely but then never says hello again. In the cafeteria I overhear him making fun of how seriously I take troubadour poems when I don't own any Dylan records. I must be the only person in the entire college who does not own a stereo, I realize. Whenever I'm on the verge of exposing too much about my origins or current arrangements to the two girls I loosely latch on to because they remind me of Carol and Ann, I exit swiftly from the conversation.

The person at school who attracts me the most is an older student, Jean, a generous, worldly woman who arrived in the United States via England and Australia. Over coffee at her house, she tells me how her mother was traumatized by the London air raids during World War II and describes her first marriage fraying at the edges before it finally unraveled. I'm surprised when she refers to her current husband as "a lovely man." He's overweight and scruffy. Then I see them cook together and during dinner he encourages me to join them for a foreign film series. After each flick, I brace for his questions, knowing I'll be gently prodded beyond "I really liked it" to developing what they call "critique." When they refer thoughtfully to things I've said about my family during previous visits, it dawns on me that they talk about me when I'm not around. For the first time in my life, I know that discussing people when they are not there doesn't necessarily involve making fun of them behind their backs.

I am happiest in the school library, shelving books for extra cash. The heavy art books drag me to the floor, where my supervisor repeatedly catches me lost in images of paintings and stunning buildings. My intellectual curiosity is as free-floating and irresistible as my anxiety. She's stymied by her obligation to reprimand me for not doing my job when I'm so eagerly doing what a lot of the other students avoid, so she shrugs her shoulders and walks away.

It is the paintings of de Chirico that become my most intimate friend; their haunted, angular spaces with solitary, undefined, tiny figures feel familiar and frightening at the same time. I wrap myself in these images as I roam Hudson River communities in Westchester County for hours at night, feeling much safer than I ever did in the Bronx. The Tudor and Georgian houses along the river are filled with happy families. Mothers, fathers and children gracefully meander through the spacious rooms I spy through backlit windows.

As soon as my scholarship money comes in, I snare an apartment by lying about age and income like a pro. Soon I value, more than college, my new cocoon: an ascetic studio apartment, furnished only with a mattress on the floor, a folding table and two chairs, two lamps and three crates. I leave books on the floor without worrying about crayon marks or cat piss.

After I spend three consecutive days totally alone, I feel like a ghost who flits back into the world of human beings only to sprinkle isolated sentences, mostly questions. Another tenant, fumbling with her mail, may hear me ask, as the elevator door closes, "Should I hold the elevator for you?" Eyeing the line filling up behind me, a cashier grimaces as I splay coins on the counter. "Do you mind if I get rid of my change?" My questions are deferred, tentative descriptions of what I cannot stop myself from doing. I'm expert at converting loneliness to solitude, clumsy at choreographing my out-of-sync steps into a social duet.

December 24, 1969, arrives to find me sitting cross-legged on the floor smoking dope I score at the local Laundromat. Suddenly there is a loud knock and through the keyhole I spy a policeman. I can't believe I'm busted on Christmas Eve. When I hesitatingly open the door, he sniffs knowingly, shaking his finger at me. "Your mother is worried about you; go home for Christmas. And you probably should not be living alone without a telephone."

Mom isn't much of a planner anymore. She didn't send the official holiday invite until Christmas Eve, when there are no buses, but at least she kept the letter I sent notifying her of my new address. I spend Christmas alone and go home the day after. An orderly house was never her priority, but I don't complain that my mother ditched the few books, papers and clothes I couldn't cart out in one trip. Instead I try to be grateful that I have been spared the fate of my humanities professor. She mused about being confronted with the inanity of her youth when her doting parents presented her with the treasure they had buried in their attic for years: her adolescent diaries, letters and favorite books, filled with exclamation points and eleven-year-old wisdom.

It doesn't take long for me to discover the major motivation for Mom inviting me back home: she fears Ralph is becoming a danger to himself. Anxious to get out of the apartment, he wanders the streets at night despite all the reports of people being killed and gang members shooting each other. Her precious nine-year-old boy is out of control, and Mom is so afraid that she has even turned to me for help. What good is college if you can't figure out how to solve a problem like a poor fatherless boy losing it minute by minute? Some drama, some higher purpose was required for Mom to let me back into the fold, which seems fair enough to me.

Mom agrees with me that she has no choice but to seek help, which comes in the form of admission to the children's ward of a state hospital. Every time we visit him during my break between semesters, he has a new bruise or cut. The heavy doses of drugs do not succeed in numbing his response to the threats and punches of the other boys on the ward, who identify him as an easy target: a white boy who doesn't know how to fight and who spends most of his time reading comic books, either alone or to a gentle six-year-old black kid they also pound and mock. "They'll kill them someday," Mom cries. She is not being hysterical.

With Jean's help I decipher the limited schedule for the local train from Penn Station to my school. Once spring semester starts I head home every other weekend, frequently staying through Monday for appointments with a social worker assigned to Ralph. With his future in common, Mom and I work smoothly as a team. If she starts to lose her temper with a confusing form or surly clerk, I calm her with a touch or a joke. I can see her now that I know I can leave her. Flicking a cigarette behind herself on the street, she's irritated that someone's feet get in the way of its landing safely in the gutter. Decades of feeling powerless have left her unaware of the repercussions of her actions. All these years I judged her for a lack of composure neither her circumstances nor her temperament made possible. She needs the kind of attention we are now scurrying to secure for her one and only son.

A tip from a nurse leads us to Jewish Philanthropies. After several meetings with me and Mom, they decide to help fund Ralph's residency at a Westchester County facility. Yes, yes, they assure her, we will respect his religious values. We're nondenominational. Mom understands the reprieve Ralph has received from this unexpected source and stops uttering the word Jew like it is a curse.

Recognizing Ralph's talent, the doctor at the new place arranges for him to work with an art therapist who will help him sculpt his own face with clay again and again until a human face replaces the monstrous figures he identifies as self-portraits. Kind men will coax him to bed and talk with him if he wakes up confused and furious. His therapist will urge Ralph to distinguish between strength and omnipotence, repeatedly reminding him he is not doomed and powerless as a result of growing up in a household of girls. For the first time in his life, Ralph will be able to turn to sane, responsible men.

Love and longing flood my consciousness when I wake from sleep thinking of my brother not allowed to leave the grounds without an escort. I worry that his psyche is in too much debt to despair to recover on its own, but try to remember he's living on a campus that impinges on him far less than the neighborhoods and family that nudged him over the edge. In a way, he has more freedom than he's ever had.

I wish there was a possibility of freedom in the future for my sister Jackie and her kid, Lisa. Not a soul was surprised when that husband of hers stopped working again, retreating to his mother and friends who would allow him to act like a baby instead of taking care of one. Jackie has tried to do the same. For the second time since she married less than two years ago, she has retreated home, cramming herself and her one-year-old daughter Lisa into one bedroom of Mom's apartment.

I'm glad Ralph's not around to hear Mom's and Jackie's war cry: "Men are such assholes." Like most slogans, it is true and not true. Unbearable pain accumulates in the vacuums created by the words we churn out in each other's presence. Maybe Ralph has cleverly found a way to escape the house and neighborhood because he's too young and beleaguered to be sustained over the long haul, as I was, by a half-baked soufflé of college dreams.

Sometimes I think that I have an obligation to stay home and help, but I suspect that I, too, would go crazy or withdraw into bed like Alice, who has become a marathon sleeper. I prefer to come and go, comfortable in my conviction that Mom's disowning me was an exaggerated gesture and always a provisional strategy. So little of her life has occurred on her terms. She had flung open the door and kicked my butt, but I sensed that she was still rooting for me, in her own way, and hoping that someday I would become a help to her and the kids.

Over tea and cigarettes at the cherry red Formica table during one weekend visit from school, we reminisce. With her child's glee that I am finally able to enjoy, she helps me fill in details about apartments and neighborhoods where we lived. I follow her cues so that we can get along. To preserve our recalibrated relationship, we have to stick to talking about our shared past. I resist mentioning *rapprochement,* even though it best explains my sense that we are melting toward one another. Mom's feelings would be hurt if I used a word she doesn't know, just as she would flinch if I explained that her fears of college were groundless—feminist essays assigned for class forced me to realize I expected impossible, Herculean support from her just because she is my mother.

It's getting easier to focus on how hard my mother tried instead of how often she failed. The memories I now share with her make her cry. "I didn't know you noticed anything good, honey," she says quietly, so I elaborate as much as I can. The more I try to please her, the more I remember.

"It's your fault I'm drawn to literature and art instead of computers and accounting," I tease her, exaggerating just a little in order to steal past her defenses. "You're the one who made me love beauty." When one of us got too loud and out of control, I tell her, you would sometimes hush us to listen to the soft sounds of music sneaking out of someone's house in the days before powerful stereo systems vied with one another.

I praise my mother for ingeniously organizing virtually costless outings. Making do with very little in those circumstances was a source of pride. Out of the apartment, in the limbo of walking, we forgot all of our arguments and worries and chattered happily.

The sense of space made it possible for us to revel in our sense of closeness. These trips were as exciting as a trip to Disneyland might be for other kids. Now several of us are indefatigable walkers, prone to wonder at people who use transportation to cover less than twenty city blocks.

When my mother joked that someone should feed all of her monkeys as well as they feed the chimpanzees at the Bronx Zoo, I heard her complaining about our demands; now I realize that, with as much humor as she could muster, she was preparing us to handle being poor. She hushes my apologies for making her feel bad about how little she could provide: "You were a child. We don't have to go over that."

Her forgiveness is a baptism. Reunited with my family, I am reborn at school. My poor choice has its compensations. Classes meet only fifteen hours a week, I work only ten, and the rest of my time is unscheduled and free of pressure. My teachers are knowledgeable, passionate and eager to bless me with A's. I can drift rather than strive. Recumbent on the floor, I read for hours in a dreamlike state, learning by osmosis rather than rote. This, finally, is peace and quiet.

Shielded from family intrusion, need and guilt, I tentatively consider citizen responsibility. There is enough time to read J. William Fulbright's concise catechism *The Arrogance of Power* twice, but no book can toughen me for public protest. Despite what I hear about the energy and oneness of young people lifting up their voices together, I feel claustrophobic and panicked in crowds. Avoiding jail and a smash to my skull matter more to me than the napalmed bodies of Vietnamese children. Politically, I prefer theory to action. Socially, I still feel most comfortable in bars.

Joan presents me with used copies of *The Female Eunuch* and *The Second Sex* and my intention to become an executive secretary vanishes, to be replaced with nothing. How selfish it would be to develop career goals now that I more fully realize our country is run by privileged men, not the democratically elected. I now understand why my mother thinks it is wrong to distinguish yourself from others. Given the opportunity to select an extraordinary talent, like a photographic memory or the ability to fly, the best I can envision for myself is acing a disability: if I should happen to go blind, I will master the art of gracefully walking into unfamiliar rooms without bumping into anything.

My mom could have chosen the dead man's float many years ago. But she splashed and kicked to stay on top of troubled waters, sputtering for help when necessary. Like her, I brace myself for a lifetime of disasters over which I will triumph. I will not let failure go to my head.

COUNTRY MUSIC, 1982

My mother now lives alone in a two-bedroom apartment in Queens, but still sleeps in the living room. Her life continues to be defined by what she can do without. Missing ovaries, a uterus, part of an intestine, and a bladder because of cancer, she deflected concern when a breast was lopped off: "It hasn't been much use to me for years." Her body is deconstructing piece by piece, just as one child after another left with little to replace them.

As if it is ceremonial tribute to a tribal king, Mom accepts the money some of us give her, but doesn't want to depend on it. Instead she scrounges around for jobs even when she is too sick to stand up, happily proving that she can operate lottery machines and a new soda fountain. "Sandy is a trouper," says the candy store owner who keeps her on call. He doesn't know that often she holes up at home, the blinds down, enveloping herself in the darkness through which Emma sees most clearly: "She is building herself a cave to die in." For years now she has stashed in the crevices of her cave—in multiples of six—socks, barrettes and spiral notebooks. Her daughters will inherit what she could not provide when we were young.

I learned from her how to make do in ways that are neurotic and resourceful. In my senior year at the State University of New York at Albany, still willfully ignorant about connections and credentials, I swiftly calculated that membership in Phi Beta Kappa wasn't worth fifteen dollars. It's not until recently, with a Ph.D. to my credit, that I've started to balk at living in hovels. I've also learned to swallow my spiky questions, even at the risk of internal bleeding, in order to preserve our fragile family peace.

If we prod Mom for clarification about her past or ours, she flees as if poked by hot needles, unable to grasp that we crave injections of truth to cure ourselves rather than to strengthen our recriminations. Some of us have been told she was abandoned as an infant in a train station, where she caught the infection that led to the removal of one eye; others that her alcoholic mother reluctantly placed her in a foster home on a temporary basis. We know she is still waiting to be retrieved from an eternity of abandonment.

On days when she flourishes, Mom teases Emma about their tumultuous relationship and praises Alice for all the time and money she has lavished on Jackie's fatherless kids. Our pictures make the rounds in the neighborhood. Every new boyfriend or girlfriend is welcomed, no questions asked. They arrive in all colors and classes, sexual preferences and job categories. "Having your health is all that matters finally," Mom says. We have no standards for distinguishing tolerance from indiscriminateness.

Several of us gather in her living room on a glorious autumn day to welcome back Ralph, who has moved home temporarily after sleeping outdoors on Virginia Beach for a couple of months. When Ralph tore out of New York, he was stressed enough to seem peculiar even to those of us accustomed to the rigidity into which he locked his body in public, inciting aggressive strangers on the street to salute him as Lurch from the Addams Family.

Staring at the door, Ralph explains his return. "Once high season was over, the cops hounded me out of town. There wasn't any more work for people like me."

Joan's recently acquired M.A. in social work is coming in handy. Gently, she probes, "It's great to have you back. We worried about you. Staying in New York for a while?"

We listen to the faucet drip and cars honk as Ralph meditates on her motives for asking and concludes she merits a staccato answer. "Alice tutors me on whatever she picks up in night school so that I can qualify for computer work. There's consulting here for someone without a degree. I'll have to stomach the city."

Mom says that Ralph is welcome to stay with her indefinitely. "Tell them about the job Lacey got to tide you over," she urges.

Because she's the bookkeeper for a large cleaning service, Lacey finagled an ideal post for Ralph: night janitor. He relishes the fact that he doesn't have to see or be seen by many people. "When someone drives me crazy calling me a honky pussy because I read computer mags during break instead of playing video games or looking at porn, I can call Lacey. She calms me, you know. She listens. We're tight."

Lacey and Ralph occasionally bond over a conviction that their intensity of alienation must mean that they are aliens from another planet. As a result of reading occult books, smoking reefer and attending séances, over the years Lacey has embraced a number of worldviews that she shares with Ralph. Everybody in this family has at least one other sibling playing mirror and coach for them. I heckled Joan back into college when she dropped out, both of us hounded Alice and Emma into GEDs and then encouraged their efforts to accrue college credits. We focus on their future; Lacey prefers to disinter evidence of our past lives as eighteenth-century royalty.

"Hey," Ralph continues, "I could come back to New York because Jackie and her brats are in Idaho. The city isn't big enough for all of us. I couldn't live here if she was stopping by all the time, smoking and carrying on about some man."

Ralph dramatically hacks and rolls his eyes, until Mom speaks. "I wish all my kids lived here. I miss my grandchildren." She circles the living room, pointing to pictures of when she and Emma visited Jackie and the kids in Idaho. "Growing up country is a hell of a lot better than growing up Bronx," she croons.

Leaning against scarred and rusted jeeps in their sun dresses, big hats and cowboy boots, following years of tortuous disentangling, Emma and Mom have reassembled into a tableau that reads: Girlfriends. After running away at fourteen and then marrying a convicted felon named Mario, Emma struck up a new relationship with Mom. She chaperones her by bus back and forth from cancer treatments and they conspire on petty food-stamp fraud. Emma pays for Mom's cigarettes in exchange for fruits and vegetables. They laugh uproariously at their favorite sitcoms and dress in the same colors before heading out to the movies. Years of kneading and stroking Mom's arthritic legs have fostered Emma's recently identified vocation as a massage therapist.

259

"Emma and I don't care what people think. We walk down the street holding hands and singing when we feel like it," Mom boasts. Right on cue, Emma encourages Mom to sing one of her very own songs.

"What songs?" Joan asks, feigning neutrality.

While Emma taps and hums, Mom's hoarse but still mellifluous voice fills the room. "I've been roaming / for a long time / I've been here and I've been there / But I know I won't breathe easy / 'Til I'm breathing / Nashville air."

Strutting a colostomy bag, a glass eye, false teeth and a wig, my mother mimes a sexy woman in her lusty prime. "We had a lovers' quarrel / As lovers sometimes do / But that's no reason to break up / And look for someone new."

After performing three of the romantic dirges she wrote, Mom drags from under the couch an upholstered box containing at least a dozen registered, sealed envelopes from and to Sandy Childers. "Poor man's copyright" is her protection from being ripped off by the producers for whom she sang her songs over the phone. "These could be worth a fortune," Emma muses.

The box also contains Jackie's colored pencil sketches of gowns designed to accommodate prosthetic devices. On top of each page is Mom's stage name, Kelli Kincaid. Joan and I learn that Lacey has agreed to serve as Mom's business manager to further protect her against sharks in the country music industry. "The competition and corruption are fierce, just like everywhere. But there are a lot of good people in the business, too, a lot of Christians," Mom explains.

Several of the songs were composed while Emma and Mom visited Idaho, inspired by all the country stations and by Jackie's promising love life. Jackie is hooked up with a guy named Sammy who lives off a nifty pension. When drunk, Sammy has a temper. When sober, he's affectionate to Jackie's son, who told his grandmother, "Sammy is the closest thing I've ever had to a father. Mom should be nicer to him, or we'll lose him." A steady paycheck and steady presence, however nonverbal, count as fatherly love even if they don't quite meet the standard of romantic love that continues to seduce his mother.

Jackie introduced Mom and Emma to her other crushes. She's in her mid-thirties and too lively to settle down with someone in his late fifties—about Mom's age—who is none too vigorous. Emma mentions that Jackie's oldest daughter, fourteen-year-old Lisa, is having an affair with a hard-drinking, hard-driving guy they have taken to calling a "real man." Lisa inherited her mom's flamboyant beauty; I reluctantly envision her flouncing her red curls and sparkling those green eyes for cowboys and other strangers.

Adeptly changing the topic, Alice prompts Emma to join her in commemorating Jackie's current main squeeze. To the tune of Bobby Hebb's hit "Sunny," Emma and Alice sing: "Sammy, thank you for the stereo you gave to me. Sammy, thank you for the house that I know is free. Sammy one so true, I'll use you." They recognize the irony of this urban crew turning to country music to express the yearning we siphon into sexuality but usually satisfy through our ragged and resilient family.

All lives are launched or derailed by circumstances, as well as by temperamental inclinations. Most of us experience a competition between the call of our best resolve and the sovereignty of our automatic selves. Nonetheless, economic and social class fundamentally influence the ways we cultivate our moments of inspiration and aspiration. In the absence of education, resources and evidence that effort pays, many poor people, such as those I love, are sustained primarily by delusion and lottery optimism. Worldviews fostered by devastating disappointments and compensatory fantasies then operate to the detriment of the poor and often at considerable cost to the society that rigidly conserves compassion. I am intimately acquainted with how lack of opportunity and personal irresponsibility can become intertwined and strangle a life. It's clear to me that I could develop from welfare brat to chip-on-the-shoulder chick to contributing, dissident citizen because I had the good luck to come of age when many people in the United States approved of a war on poverty rather than what Herbert J. Gans calls "the war against the poor."

AUTHOR'S NOTE

This book consists primarily of episodes in my childhood and adolescence. Out of concern for the privacy of others, names have been changed and identities disguised. To enliven the narrative, I merge a few events in time, leap and fill in gaps in memories about sequence and details, and reconstruct dialogue I could not possibly remember verbatim. I am grateful to my sisters for helping me unearth what they prefer to leave untouched and indebted to many others who encouraged this project, particularly my husband, Bruce L. Levine; the Rockefeller Foundation Bellagio Center; and my friends Daniel Cottom, Michael T. Gilmore and Marianne Hirsch. Thanks to the conviction of my agent, Elisabeth Weed, and the acute challenges of my editor, Gillian Blake, the chain of memories rattling in my head settled into a narrative.

A NOTE ON THE TYPE

The text of this book is set in Adobe Caslon, named after the English punch-cutter and type founder William Caslon I (1692–1766). Caslon's rather old-fashioned types were modeled on seventeenth-century Dutch designs, but found wide acceptance throughout the English-speaking world for much of the eighteenth century until being replaced by newer types toward the end of the century. Used in 1776 to print the Declaration of Independence, they were revived in the nineteenth century, and have been popular ever since, particularly among fine printers. There are several digital versions, of which Carol Twombly's Adobe Caslon is one.